The Catchy Clarinet Book of CHRISTMAS CAROLS

41 Traditional Christmas Carols arranged especially for Clarinet.

Mostly below the break.

Play-Along Backing Tracks and Piano Accompaniment book available online!

Amanda Oosthuizen
Jemima Oosthuizen

The Catchy Clarinet Series
Wild Music Publications
www.wildmusicpublications.com

We hope you enjoy *The Catchy Clarinet Book of Christmas Carols!*

We have loads more books for you,
such as: *Christmas Duets, 50+ Greatest Classics,
Trick or Treat – A Halloween Treat, Easy Duets from Around the
World, Moonlight and Roses, Intermediate Classic Duets,*
and many more!

To see what you might be missing out on, visit:
http://WildMusicPublications.com

Visit our secret page for a **free backing track,**
and more fun things for free! visit:

http://WildMusicPublications.com/553secret-tracks65-clarinet754/

And use the password: **m@DWinds4U**

Happy Music-Making!

The Wild Music Publications Team

To keep up –to-date with our new releases, why not
follow us on Twitter

@WMPublications

© Copyright 2016 Wild Music Publications

The music in this book is protected by copyright and may not be reproduced in any way for sale or private use without the consent of the author.

Contents

Page

Angels from the Realms of Glory 12
Away in a Manger 5
Boar's Head Carol 14
Carol of the Drum 19
Cherry Tree Carol 15
Coventry Carol 8
Deck the Halls 10
Ding Dong Merrily on High 11
Down in Yon Forest 17
Drive the Cold Winter Away 20
Gloucestershire Wassail 19
God Rest Ye Merry Gentlemen 4
Good King Wenceslas 2
Hark! The Herald Angels Sing 6
Il Est Ne, Le Divin Enfant 21
In Dulci Jubilo 17
Infant Holy, Infant Lowly 18
In the Bleak Midwinter 22
I Saw Three Ships 13
It Came Upon a Midnight Clear 6
Jingle Bells 2
Jingle Bells (Full version) 22
Joy to the World 12
O'Carolan's Lament 20
O Come All Ye Faithful 3
O Come, O Come Emmanuel 18
O Little Town of Bethlehem 11
Once in Royal David's City 7
Past Three O'clock 8
Pat-a-Pan 21
Sans Day Carol 16
See Amid the Winter's Snow 14
Silent Night 3
Sussex Carol 16
The First Nowell 7
The Holly and the Ivy 9
The Wexford Carol 13
Twelve Days of Christmas 10
Wassail Song 15
We Three Kings 4
We Wish You a Merry Christmas 9
While Shepherds Watched 5

Away in a Manger

While Shepherds Watched

The Holly and the Ivy

We Wish You a Merry Christmas

Sans Day Carol

Sussex Carol

In the Bleak Midwinter

Jingle Bells

Joyful and Jolly!

If you have enjoyed **The Catchy Clarinet Book of Christmas Carols**, why not try the other books in the **Catchy Clarinet** series!

For more info, please visit: **WildMusicPublications.com**

All of our books are available to download, or you can order from Amazon.

Introducing some of our favourites:

Champagne and Chocolate

50+ Greatest Classics

Trick or Treat – A Halloween Suite

More Christmas Duets

Easy Traditional Duets

Christmas Bonanza

Easy Duets from Around the World

Christmas Duets

Moonlight and Roses

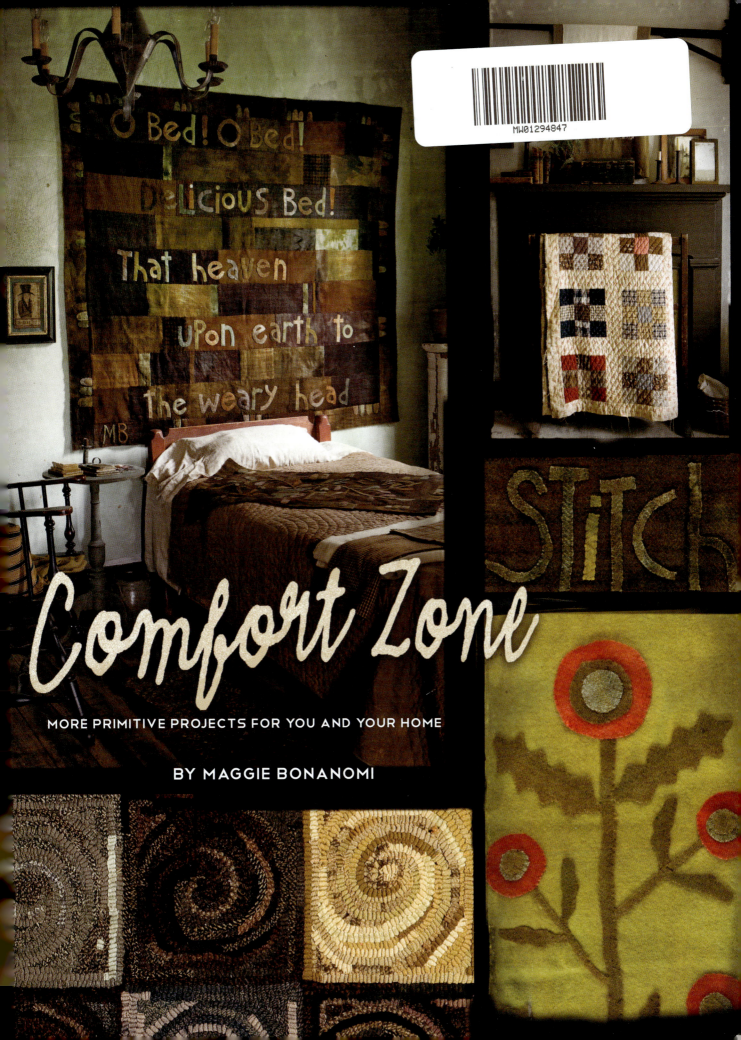

Comfort Zone

MORE PRIMITIVE PROJECTS FOR YOU AND YOUR HOME

BY MAGGIE BONANOMI

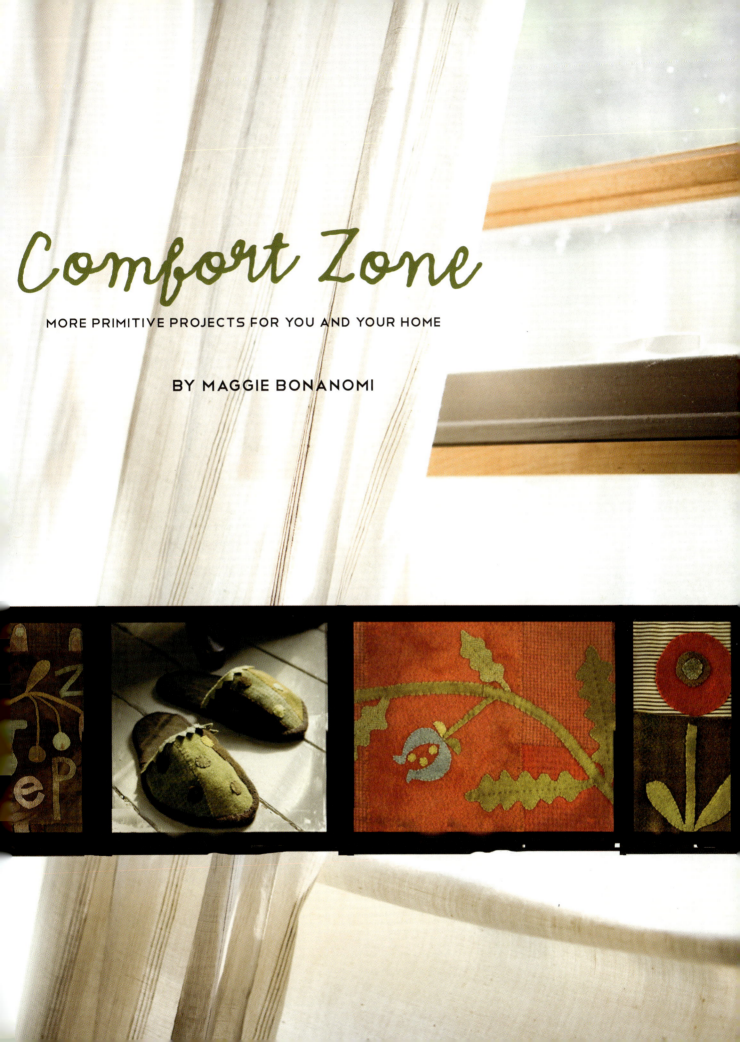

Comfort Zone

MORE PRIMITIVE PROJECTS FOR YOU AND YOUR HOME

BY MAGGIE BONANOMI

Comfort Zone

MORE PRIMITIVE PROJECTS
FOR YOU AND YOUR HOME

BY MAGGIE BONANOMI

Editor: Deb Rowden
Designer: Brian Grubb
Photography: Aaron T. Leimkuehler
Illustration: Maggie Bonanomi and
 Lon Eric Craven
Technical Editor: Nan Doljac
Production Assistance: Jo Ann Groves

Published by:
Kansas City Star Books
1729 Grand Blvd.
Kansas City, Missouri, USA 64108

All rights reserved
Copyright © 2010 The Kansas City Star Co.

No part of this book may be reproduced, stored in a retrieval system, or transmitted in any form or by any means, electronic, mechanical, photocopying, recording or otherwise, without the prior consent of the publisher. Exception: we grant permission to photocopy the patterns for personal use only.

No finished quilts or other projects featured in this book can be produced or sold commercially without the permission of the author and publisher.

First edition, first printing
ISBN: 978-1-935362-49-4

Library of Congress Control Number:
2010929562

Printed in the United States of America by Walsworth Publishing Co., Marceline, MO

To order copies, call StarInfo at
(816) 234-4636 and say "Books."

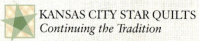

www.PickleDish.com

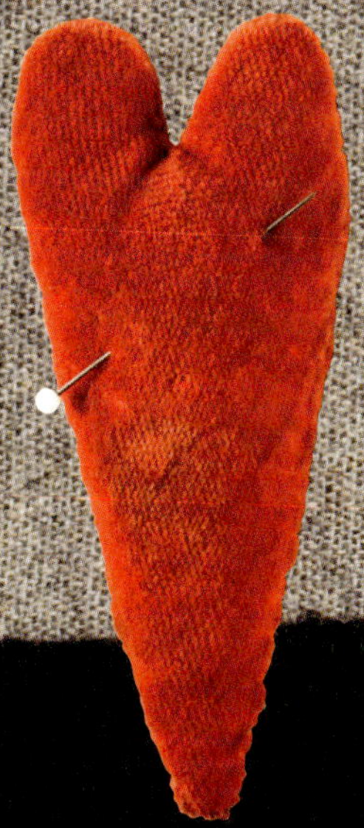

Contents

Projects

Crazy Wool Comfort	16
Urn #10 Wool Pillow	23
Initially Yours Pillow	28
Sewing Circle	30
Toe Warmers/Wool Slippers	34
Simplify Wool Mat	40
O Bed! Bed Cover	46
Sleep Pillow Cover	54
Urn Full of Flowers Appliquéd Mat	60
Black Wool Pomegranate Tablerunner	66
Red Wool Runner with Pomegranates	70
PINS Pincushion	72
Stitch Rollups	74
Crazy Wool Jacket	80
Pins (for your Jacket)	88
Colored Blocks Hooked Rug	92
Primitive Ovals Hooked Rug	96
Square in a Square Hooked Rug	106
Resources	111

Acknowledgements	6
Dedication	6
About the Author	7
Introduction	8
Comfort Zone	10
It's Distressing	11
Useful and Necessary	12

Acknowledgements

First I must again thank Diane McLendon and Doug Weaver of Kansas City Star Books for the opportunity to do another book.

Thanks to:

My friends in "wool" - I have met many along the way: Emma Lou Lais who inspired me to begin rug hooking; Rhonda Manley and her wonderful studio and wool at Black Sheep Design Studio; as well as the gals at hooking that continue to keep me on task.

Cindi and Tonja at Blackberry Primitives for dyeing and shipping me wool (even as they are heading to market).

My friend Jeanne Horton at Country Sampler in Spring Green, Wisconsin for your friendship, continued support and great workshops. You bring together a great bunch of gals and I don't know where else I laugh so much.

Rita Briner at Quilter's Station in Lee's Summit, Missouri for your shop full of wonderful fabrics and wool to inspire a project, and a great place to teach at your annual Primitives of the Midwest.

Pam and Janet at Buggy Barn, in Reardan, Washington. You keep asking me back to do what I want at your workshops.

My friend Michelle Neer for putting up with me period, but also with letting me test out my Crazy Wool Jacket - and for her handsome cat Kiki for inspiring a little bit of whimsy.

My friend Pat Worth, who owns a wonderful independent book store here in Lexington. You always find me a great read when I need a break, provide great coffee and a place for friends to gather - and always have a wonderful place for my book signing, thank you for all you do..

Deb Rowden, my editor, I feel lucky to work with you again. You do all the important things to make my writing come together. I appreciate your friendship and support and your patience! We do make a good team, thank you.

Aaron Leimkuehler, my photographer, you are great to work with and your photos are the best. Brian Grubb, my book designer, you make my book look wonderful. I am very happy you both are on my team, thank you for all you do.

Eric Lon Craven, my illustrator, and Nan Doljac, my technical editor, thanks for all you do to make the patterns and pieces all come together as they should.

Jo Ann Groves, my production assistant, thanks for what you do and thank you for helping lug my project models in to The Star.

I cannot forget my friends here in Lexington. We are a small town filled with big friendships. Thanks for your continued hand holding and support as I work - and an occasional viewing of a project in progress - for me, this is what makes Lexington home.

Thanks of course, to my family. I could not do this without your love and support.

And to all of you - those I have had the pleasure to meet and those I have not yet met, thank you. Without your wonderful support of my books, design work and workshops, this would not be possible.

Dedication

I dedicate this to my family who provide the comfort of love and understanding - and even a little tolerance!

About the Author

I still feel awfully lucky to live and work doing what I love to do, creating with fabric, textures and color and living here in Lexington, Missouri in my wonderful old house that makes the perfect backdrop for my projects.

I grew up moving around, as my dad was in the Air Force. There were three of us kids that packed up our toys while mother packed up our home and off we went to our new location. We lived in California, Washington, from the Midwest to New England, always having to start over again. We did it. I used this great lesson when I married and my husband decided to return to the Army for another 20 years. We spent time moving stateside but also had two tours in Germany. I always wanted to make our home comfortable but we often did not have much of our own furniture with us. So, I used lessons learned from my mother, making do with what we had and creating comfort in what was available to us - a good lesson in creativity that I still draw on today.

I am thankful I have had many interesting opportunities to create and design and best of all, an outlet for it. With our move some eight years ago to this home in Missouri, my focus has become more defined. Clearly the 19th century fits me and my home. I hope to stay here for a long time, it suits me just fine.

I used lessons learned from my mother, making do with what we had and creating comfort in what was available to us - a good lesson in creativity that I still draw on today.

Introduction

Comfort is the theme of this book, especially your own comfort zone. That's where you are comfortable working with color or subject - or take comfort from the finished project. Who wants to step out of theirs? I seem to stick very close to my own comfort zone.

Comfortable projects you'll find inside:

The **Crazy Wool Comfort** is just that, a bit crazy using old clothing and leftover wool. It becomes warm comfort on a cold night.

The **Urn #10 Wool Pillow** adds a little leaf and urn project to break up the strong lines of the wool comfort.

The **Initially Yours** project is simple: add your initial or someone else's to this simple but graphic pillow.

The **Sewing Circle** is a sweet little addition to your sewing necessities. Appliqué with a little wool to decorate the outside, then fold it up and tie it closed with a piece of ribbon.

The **Toe Warmers** are wool slippers made to do just that. Use wools you have and decorate these as you wish.

Simplify is a good word to live by. This mat - placed on a table or chest - is a good reminder of that.

The **O Bed! Bed Cover** was fun to make. I love to use words in my work and love what this one says, particularly after a long day of work. It is a great size to use on your bed but great to wrap up in as well.

The **Sleep Pillow Cover** was made to go with the O Bed! Bed Cover. Its' another place to feature an urn and some leaves. Use it to cover your pillow or a table nearby

The **Urn Full of Flowers Appliquéd Mat** is on a nubby raw silk. It would be equally great on linen, wool or cotton. We hung it on my new white cupboard - you could frame this or make a pillow out of it.

When it comes to sewing, you can never have too many sewing necessities, the **Pins Pincushion** is filled with grit. That will help it set dutifully on the table or chair arm to hold your pins and needle. The **Sewing Rollup** is another place for safekeeping your sewing items while the **Hooking Rollup** will serve the rug hooker. Both rollups are adorned with wool appliqué. Mix or match the designs of each, as they are the same size.

The **Wool Pomegranate Tablerunners** show two ways to do the same design – one dark colors, the other (a step out of my comfort zone) in red.

The **Crazy Wool Jacket** was designed to give warmth and have some fun as well. I made one for myself and one for my friend Michelle since she allowed me to use her as a manikin for the project.

The **three hooked rugs** are each inspired by antique rugs that were made from all kinds of fabric besides wool - I used just wool. I love their graphic style and how each original was designed with a limited palate of color and still came up with a pleasing design and the basic need of comfort was accomplished in the end, no cold toes.

I hope you try out these projects and find your own comfort zone - whether it is in the process of stitching or rug hooking, color choice or just in the end result: a warm bed, a jacket or just some comfy warm toes.

9 Comfort Zone

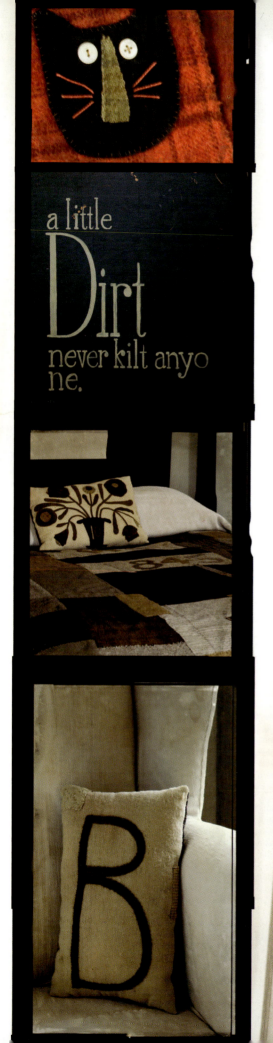

Comfort Zone

Comfort-to give sense of ease; person or thing that comforts, state of ease and quiet enjoyment, any thing that makes life easy or comfortable, quilted bed covering.

That dictionary definition pretty well covers the idea of a comfort zone for me. When I began to work on this book, I had a different plan in mind, always including what I love to do but with a little different twist to things – leaving my comfort zone. As I tried to step out of my comfort zone, it became apparent that I kept stepping back into it where I seem to be firmly entrenched.

We seek comfort in many things. The first is family and friends, our homes, food and clothing. In our homes, it may be a cozy bed to sleep in, a favorite chair to sit on to stitch or read. Maybe it is just being warm or cool, depending on the season. We often surround ourselves with things we love that provide comfort. Food can be a comfort, for me, a great cup of coffee and some chocolate are a couple of things that fall into that category. Clothing! We all have things we love to wear (and there are things we feel uncomfortable in).

We are fortunate to live in a time when we can go to stores or buy from catalogs or online to get what we need. In the past, you needed to make these things if you wanted to be warm when you went to bed or have warm toes when you stepped out of bed. Old clothing and scraps were used to make quilts and comforts - even hooked rugs. I love the history that goes along with this and I try to recreate this feeling, but I am also happy it is not the reality today. Life today is much easier.

Color is another of my comfort zones. Maybe this falls into 'the state of ease and quiet enjoyment' defined by the dictionary. I am asked why I choose to use dark colors. I think they are rich. They just appeal to me and are calming. I enjoyed working with different color combinations and love the result but I find I return to what I love best. Any of these projects can be done in any colors. Choose what puts you in your comfort zone - just substitute your choice for the colors given.

It's Distressing

Or how to add an aged look to your projects...

I like the aged look in my projects and prefer using old fabrics to achieve this. When you cannot find these fabrics, visit your quilt shop for a wonderful supply of reproduction cottons, linen and cotton linen blends - often wool as well.

Wool can be aged by just snipping or cutting a few places randomly on the surface, then fraying the edges. Wool also tears - if you fray or fringe the edge, it will add some age. I often use the holes and frayed edges of old wool as design elements in my projects. If you find an old Army blanket, a white blanket, or other wool that is damaged (even with moth holes), you can use it. However, be absolutely sure there is no current infestation. Wash it as soon as you get it home.

Antiquing your fabric can be done with Rit dye, or with walnut ink or crystals. Always wet your fabric first and lay it on a foil or parchment paper covered cookie sheet. Lightly apply the solution and add more if needed. I usually mix up my dye of walnut crystal in a small bowl, and dilute as needed. Scrunch up the fabric so it gives random coverage. I dry small projects in the oven at about 200 degrees. You do need to keep on eye on this - do not dry any combustible fabric this way. You can also dye with old coffee or coffee grounds as well as tea.

Add a patch whether needed or not.

Ribbon can look too stiff on a project. I prefer silk or rayon ribbons. I find if I dampen them and scrunch them up, even tying them while damp, it will add age. Be sure to check for colorfastness as hand-dyed ribbon might bleed color onto your project.

Old looking pins make pincushions appear older. To make your pins look older, dye them. Heat up some water, add liquid tan Rit dye and pour it into a glass jar. The amount of dye should be fairly strong. Then add a box of plastic headed quilt pins. Let them soak until the heads are as dark as you wish. Empty the jar using a sieve so no pins go down your drain, then rinse them and lay them on paper towels to dry. Do not use any jar or sieve you use for dyeing for food.

These are just a couple of things that will add age to your projects. Experiment and see what works for you.

Useful and Necessary

Here are things I like to have on hand, along with a few helpful hints to make working on projects a bit easier.

Hand-sewing supplies

Needles (your choice)

Scissors for cutting fabric as well as ones for cutting paper, a small pair to snip seams or project pieces

Pins

Tape measure

Thread (I like Coats and Clark thread summer brown, black and ecru)

Walnut ink or crystal for aging fabric

A collection of favorite fabrics: wools and pieces of old textiles, linen, velvet, old calico and cotton homespun

Ribbon and trims

Old buttons - shell or bone

Cotton or wool stuffing (cotton balls are good for small projects)

Cotton batting: thin or cotton flannel

Other helpful items

An old Army blanket is great for a background or appliqué, even for hooking

Freezer paper to transfer patterns

Quilters rule - my favorite is 6 1/2" x 13"

Rotary cutting mat - great to place under projects as you stitch (particularly large ones) to protect your table surface

Liquid Rit tan dye for aging fabric

A big magnet for gathering up spilt pins! This may seem silly but we have a magnet on a long handle. After a roofing project, it was used to find nails in the yard. It is the best pin-picker-upper, especially if you have space between the boards of an old floor.

These are just some things that I think are necessary and useful to have on hand if you get inspired to make something. When I travel, I take along some fabrics and my hand sewing supplies to keep me busy in the hotel. It reminds me of the bags of things I'd fix for my girls' entertainment on long trips (except they had kid stuff).

Of course, having your favorite quilt shop and wool studio nearby helps as well.

Measuring curves

Here's an easy way to measure something that is curved. Instead of doing the math to find the circumference of something, I use a piece of string or yarn. First, lay it along the edge of what you need to measure. Then place it along the straight edge of your quilters rule or tape measure. I use this method to determine the amount of edging I need or the length of a stem or branch in a project.

13 Comfort Zone

Projects

Crazy Wool Comfort

Crazy Wool Comfort

A Primitive Wool Bed Cover
77" x 88"

Old wool quilts or comforts were made from worn clothing and scraps, providing a cozy comfortable way to ward off the cold winter wind. I have seen many over the years in antique shops or sales. Some were so heavy I could not imagine if you tucked the kids in at night that they would ever be able to get out of bed till you came in the next morning and lifted it off them.

My inspiration for this piece was an old wool crazy comfort I bought years ago. It had fairly primitive embroidery stitching around the different blocks of wool, as well as being tied at regular intervals. I love the old piece but wanted the wool to be the main attraction of my crazy wool comfort.

I have drawn up a chart for you to refer to but please understand that it is not precise. The comfort is not made up of exact squares but of wool pieces set down in vertical panels. The measurements on the chart are approximate: my center panel was about 19 1/2" wide at the top but further down was more like 20 1/2".

The colors are what I assembled for this project: black, grays, oatmeal color, rust, Army green, tans, plaids, striped, tweeds etc. A trip to the thrift store, garage sale or just your own closet will be a place to start - just be sure you wash any clothing you use first. The fact that clothing is used will also vary the amount of wool you have in a given color. For some, this will pose no problem but for those of you wanting exact measurements it is a good project to step out of your particular comfort zone. Just refer to the chart, allowing some extra for 1/4" overlaps of wool.

Another thing to think about is that *no two scraps will be the same size.* As I laid out the panels working from center to the left edge then to the right edge, I filled in any gap with a patch of wool. A few patches cover holes in old clothing. Some I just put there to break up too large an area of one color. I pieced some of the blocks of one color together to get the size I wanted. This practice is not new - look at examples of old quilts and you will see how thrifty our predecessors were.

Although I designed this for wool, I do know not everyone lives where wool is necessary or very comfortable. You can use other fabrics such as old denim, flannel, used cotton clothing, and so on.

Fabric requirements and supplies

Note: these are approximate, but give you something to start with. I have assigned a letter code to the colors so you will see where they are used in this project according to the chart.

Muslin - 5 yards for foundation
Black stripe ticking - 5 yards for backing
A - black wool 1 yard for border

The following fabrics make up the comfort top

A - black wool 1 yard scraps/clothing
B - rust check hand-dyed wool 1/4 yard
C - charcoal stripe wool skirt
D - oatmeal wool 1/2 yard
E - black stripe wool skirt
F - gray tweed wool skirt
G - tan plaid wool 1/8 yard
H - Army blanket (approximately 1/2 blanket)
I - gray wool slacks
J - tan wool pants
K - rusty/black dyed plaid wool 1/8 yard
L - gray plaid wool 1/8 yard
M - solid rust dyed wool 1/8 yard
N - dark gray wool skirt
P - gray stripe wool slacks
Q - 3" square brown check cotton homespun patch
Coats and Clark summer brown and black thread
*Optional - black perle cotton

*O Bed! O Bed! delicious bed
That heaven upon earth
to the weary head —*

— Thomas Hood

Cutting/Assembly

Divide the prewashed muslin into 2 - 2 1/2 yard pieces - join them to have a piece 2 1/2 yards x approximately 80". (Note: this depends on how much the muslin shrunk.) Use this center seam as center of the comfort - begin with your center panel (the 19" wide one). Use the patterns provided for the date 1845 on page 20, or make up your own date or initials. Use scraps, appliqué in place.

Lay out the wool pieces then baste them in place, working all the way down before going on to the next panel. Fill in with patches so there are no 'seams' - just overlap the wools about 1/4".

After the crazy comfort was assembled, I added stitching with black thread to each block before I put the backing on. I say stitch because it isn't fine like quilt stitching. I filled the spaces with big x's and zig-zags as well as a curvy line and even a spiral. Here is where the *optional black thread comes in. It's hard to see the stitching on the top although I promise you it is there. If you want it to show up, use perle cotton.

Once you have completed all that, add the border. I tore the wool into 4" wide lengths. Occasionally I pieced in a patch or two (see chart, top and bottom borders are 4" x 70" with 1/2" seam allowance, the border is joined only along one seam leaving a 3 1/2" border. The side borders are made the same - they are 4" x 88", again, lay the border 1/2" under the sides leaving a 3 1/2" border, stitch all around.

Piece the backing together as desired - be sure it is 1" larger all around to allow enough to turn in between the wool and backing. It is not necessary to turn in the raw edge of the border. Stitch all along the edge of the border, securing front to back. If you desire, stitch in the ditch thru all layers where the panels join to secure the back to the front.

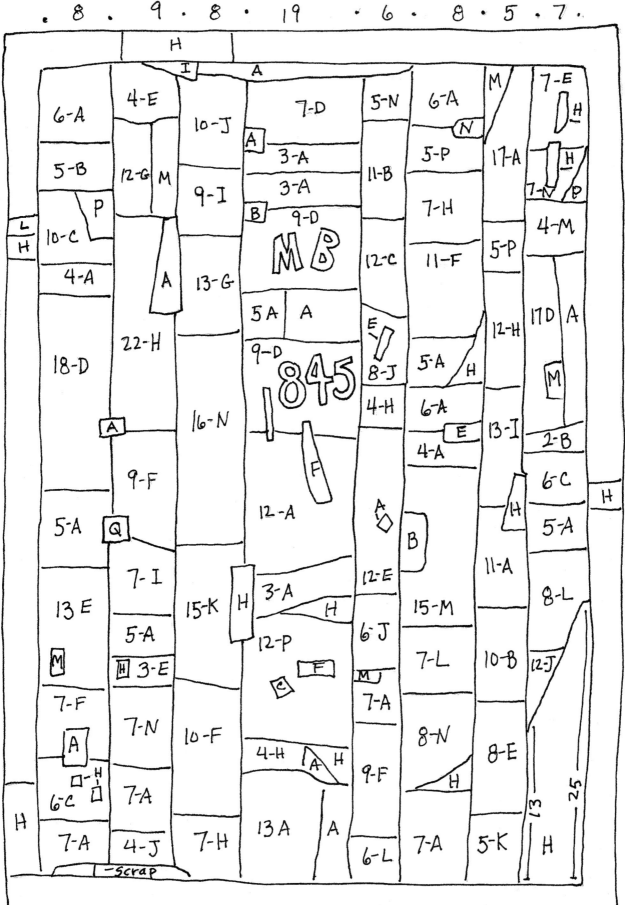

Urn #10 Wool Pillow

18" x 13"

This pillow was designed to go with the Crazy Wool Comfort. I felt the need to see a leaf or two after all the blocks of wool of the comfort. I like the funny black urn that reminds me of an old iron mortar I have. The #10 is for the year 2010 but can be whatever you want. The bouquet is an odd bunch of flowers but I like them. For the pillow front, I used wool from an old blanket. If you do not have access to some old flawed wool, read how to distress your wool on page 11.

Fabric requirements and supplies

Antique white wool 19" x 14" for pillow front
Black cotton calico 19" x 14" for pillow back
Black wool 8" x 6" for urn, flower parts
Natural/gray check wool 2" x 4" for flower, heart bud, #1, flower part
Brown wool 5" x 10" for flowers
Medium brown wool 4" square for flower, #0
Army green wool 8" x 13" for stems, leaves, flower bases
Mustard wool 2" x 3" for flower centers
Brown check cotton homespun 2" x 3 1/2" for patch
Cotton stuffing
Coats and Clark summer brown thread
Hand sewing supplies

Cutting/Assembly

First, center the urn 1" above the edge of the long side of the pillow front. Refer to the diagram and the photo to lay out the rest of the appliqué pieces. Next add the stems using the diagram for stem lengths - they are cut 1/4" wide or narrower, with ends tucked under the urn rim. The flowers are lettered from left to right beginning with "A" with information on the pattern pieces. Flowers "C" and "G" have fringe cut along one edge of the pattern piece labeled 'fringe' with the uncut edge tucked under the adjacent piece. For flower "B", I used a frayed piece of wool as part of the flower. The black wool around the mustard center is actually the irregular selvage edge from my wool. You can cut an irregular strip to use here (if you do not have some selvage, you will need about a 6" long piece). When you have arranged the appliqué pieces, stitch them down with a simple whip stitch.

Assemble the pillow

Place the appliquéd pillow front and black cotton calico back right sides together. Using 1/2" seams, stitch around 3 sides. Turn right side out and stuff with cotton stuffing - do not make it too puffy. Flatten the pillow some as you stuff, then turn in open edges and stitch closed. Add a brown check cotton homespun patch along the lower right hand side.

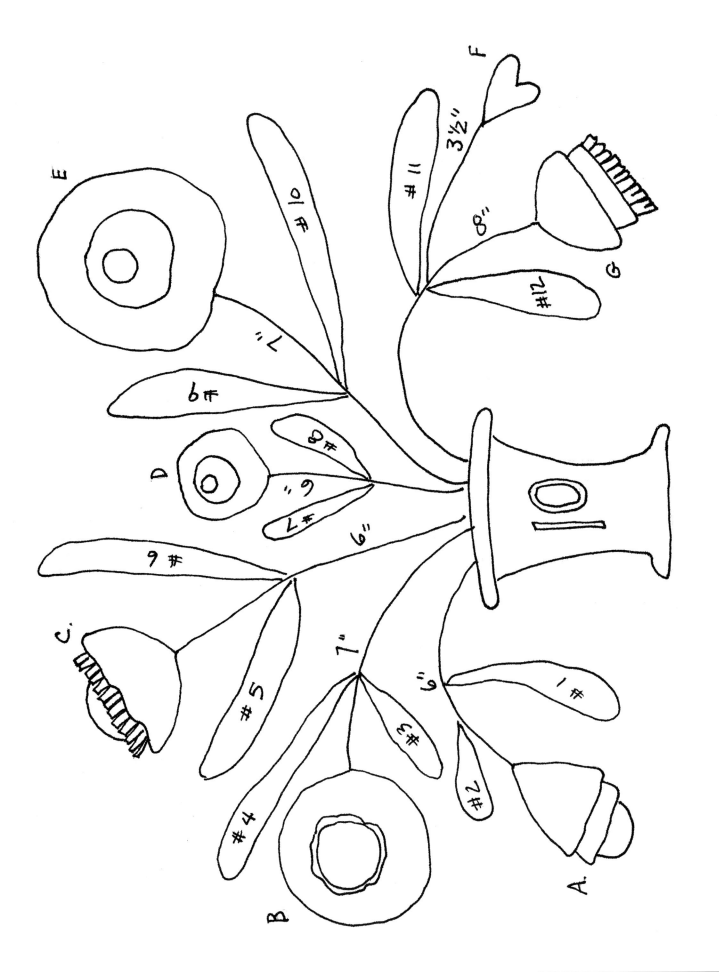

25 Comfort Zone

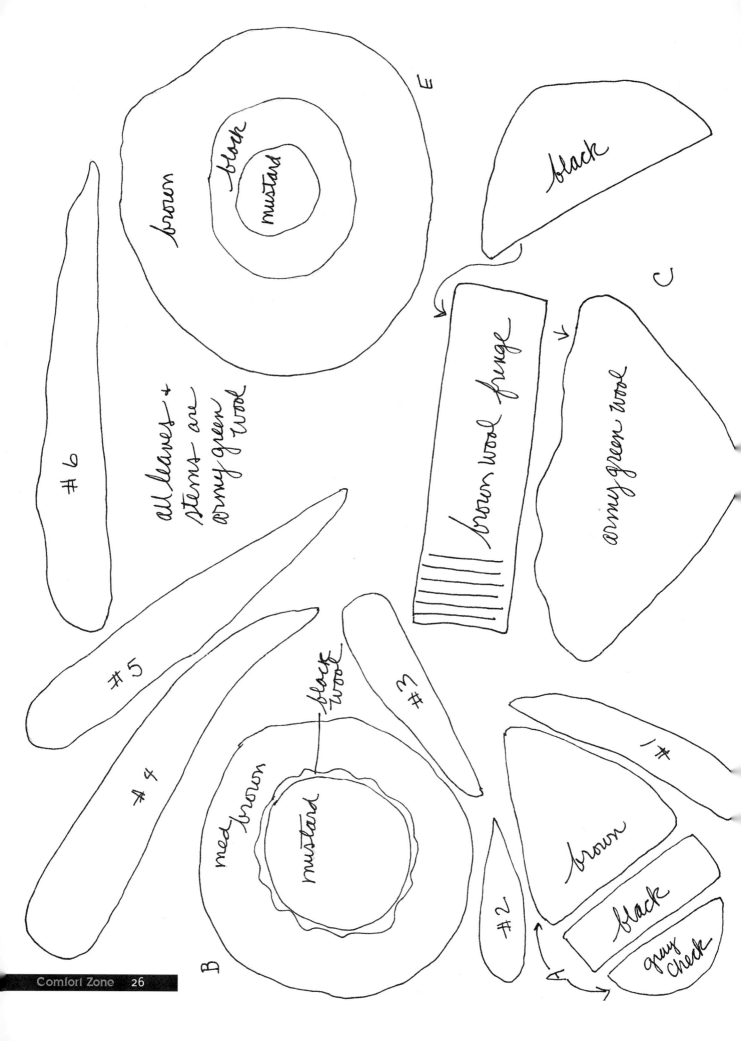

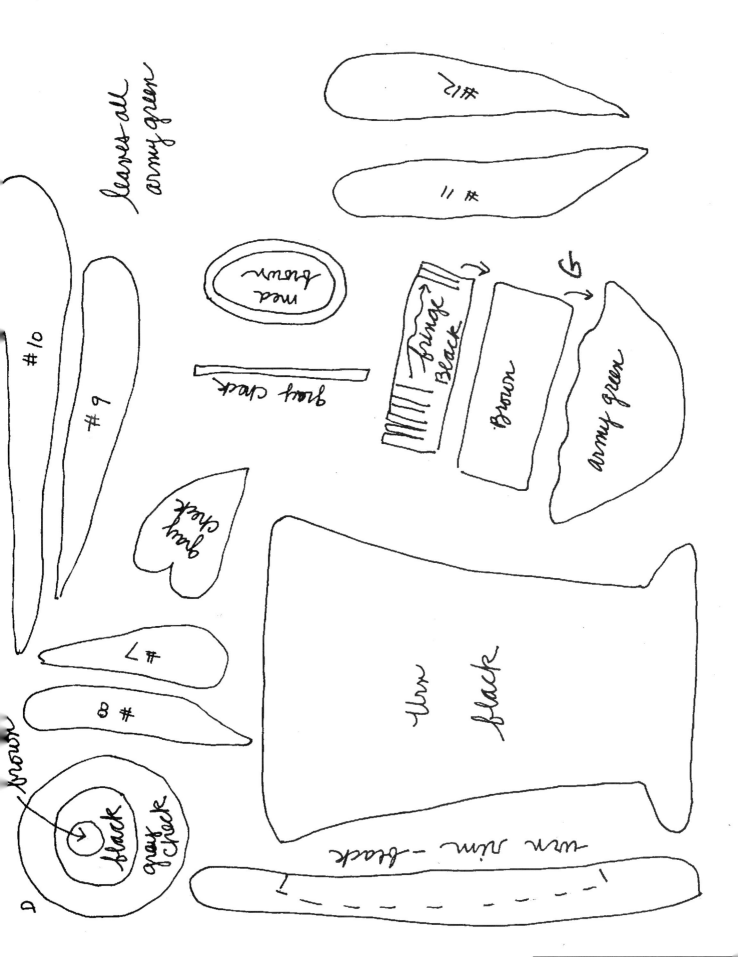

Initially Yours

Wool Letter Pillow

9" x 13"

This little wool project uses your initial or any letter or number you choose. This is a fun pillow to add to your pillow collection. You could do one for any family member, kids or grandkids, even college kids. Create these simple "stick" letters using 1/2" wide wool strips. I used a greeny brown but you can use any color, even mixing colors in one letter.

This pillow was made with a piece of antique white wool blanket but any antique white wool will work. I discuss aging and distressing your wool on page 11 - to add years to your new wool.

Fabric requirements and supplies

- Antique white wool 10" x 14" for pillow front (adjust if you have a wider letter)
- Black cotton calico 10" x 14" for pillow back (adjust if you have a wider letter)
- Browny green wool approximately 32" x 1/2"* letter
- *Note: this size will vary depending on which letter you are using and can be pieced together as needed
- Brown and white check cotton homespun, scrap 2" x 3 1/2"
- White wool scrap 2" square, patch
- Cotton stuffing
- Coats and Clark summer brown thread
- Hand sewing supplies

Create the letter

Plan your letter. Use a sheet of paper if desired and make it about 10" high. Draw out your initial and use this as a guide to form your letter. Start with any straight parts, pinning in place. Add the curved or rounded parts next, tucking in any ends as needed. When I made the "B", I placed the straight line first, then added the 2 rounded parts, tucking under the strips where they meet. Once it was all pinned down, I stitched the straight part first, then stitched the outer edge of the rounded parts. The inside curves need to be eased in gently.

Assembly

To assemble the pillow, place the calico back and appliquéd pillow front right sides together. Stitch around 3 sides, then turn it right-side out and stuff. Turn under the remaining edges and stitch the opening closed.
Add a cotton patch on the side and wool patch in upper left corner if desired.

Sewing Circle

A Sweet Little Sewing Kit

10 1/2" when open, 5" x 7" folded

The name "Sewing Circle" reminds me of a group of women (usually) that gathers together in homes or church basements to enjoy each other's company, as well as often sewing for a common cause or interest. I think now the term guild is used, as in quilt guild. The comfort of spending time with others having the same interest is something that does not go out of style.

This sewing circle is a functional little project as well as something that looks good. It will lay nicely on the arm of a chair or on the table close at hand. It folds up and is tied closed with some silk ribbon, leaving a little appliqué and shell buttons showing.

Fabric requirements and supplies

Prewashed white linen, cotton linen or textured cotton 11" square for outside

Prewashed reproduction cotton shirting with black shapes 11" square for lining

Prewashed white cotton flannel 10" square for batting

Black wool 31" x 1/2" for edging*

   *Optional: if you have a wonderful length of crochet edging, it can be used here

Linen 2" x 4" for the words "stitch, stitch, stitch"

White wool 2" x 3 1/2" for needlekeep

Silk ribbon, 1 yard for ties/inside tie

Linen 5" square for inside pocket

Black wool scrap for heart, stem, leaves, initial

Brown wool scrap for flower, initial, leaf and stem

8 - 1/4" shell buttons for flower center, berries

Coats and Clark summer brown and Ecru thread

Black permanent/waterproof ink pen (such as Pigma pens) for words

Walnut ink for antiquing

Cutting/Assembly

Make a pattern for a 10 1/2" circle. I used a dinner plate but have provided a partial pattern for you to use on page 33. Cut out 2 circles: one from linen and one from shirting.

If you want to antique your fabric, do it now along with the ribbon and additional linen and white wool piece. See page 11 on how to do this. Doing the antiquing now eliminates any non colorfast dark wool from bleeding into the surrounding fabric. (I found out I had some non colorfast black wool.)

Cut out a 9 1/2" circle of white flannel. Use ecru thread and stitch 1/2" around the inside edge of the linen piece. Carefully clip the curve, then lay the flannel in the center. Press the clipped edge down over the edge of the flannel, lay the cotton shirting on top (right side up), and pin in the center to hold it in place. Turn back 1/2" of the shirting so the two fabrics (cotton and linen) are the same size. Pin.

Comfort Zone

Take the wool strip and clip along one edge (about every 1/2"), leaving one side uncut. Once that is complete, go back and round off the sections so you now have a strip of scallops. See the edging diagram on page 33. Pin the strip around the edge between the linen and the shirting. Here I used the ecru thread, first stitching the linen side to the scalloped edging then the inside.

Fold the circle into quarters with the shirting on the inside. Gently finger press it to lightly set the fold lines. Follow the photo to arrange the heart, initials, flower and sprig with button berries. When stitching in place, be sure not to go through to the shirting side.

On the shirting side, add these items in the quarters of the circle:

1. The wool rectangle for a needlekeep.
2. Stitch the middle 1" of a 12" length of ribbon in the next quarter.
3. Make a pocket by first turning down 1/4" then again the pocket top edge and stitch finished pocket edge, now turn the sides under 1/4" and stitch in one of the quarters trim any excess fabric. Use ecru thread.
4. Take the 2"x 4" linen piece and write Stitch, Stitch, Stitch. Turn the raw edges under 1/4" all around and stitch to last quarter of the sewing circle, then top stitch with the summer brown thread.

Fold the circle into fourths. You can decide what designs show, once folded. Stitch the remaining ribbon, cut in two, to the two folded edges just down from the scalloped edge. Tie into a bow.

Comfort Zone

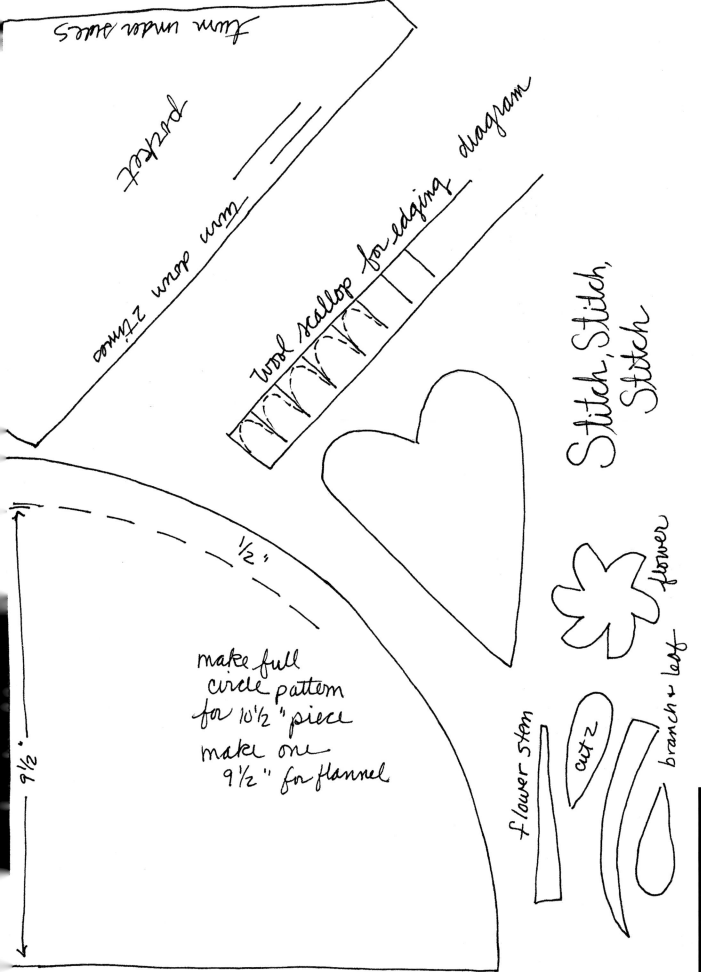

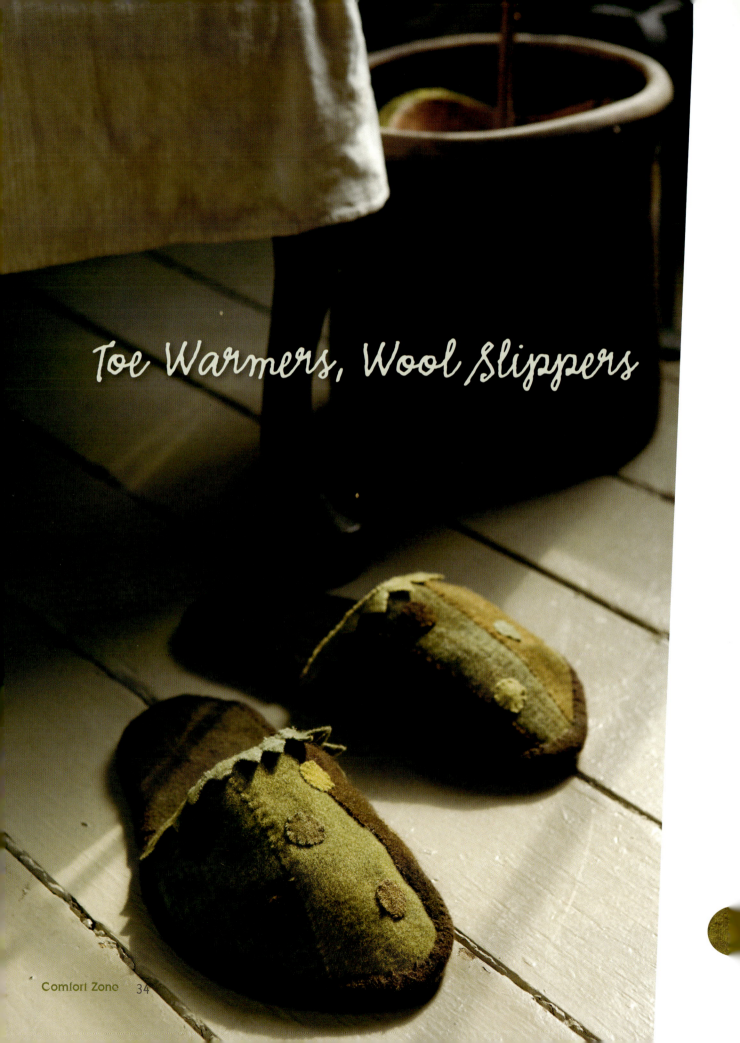

Toe Warmers, Wool Slippers

What can be more comforting than warm toes?

These slippers are just that, toe warmers. A fun way to keep your toesies warm while stitching, reading or rug hooking - not so much for walking around the house. I live in an old house and the winters are pretty cold, but I have also been in air conditioning and was happy to have my toes covered! I have used wool from an old Army blanket as part of the "structure" of the slipper and then some dyed wools as the decorative part. They are designed so each slipper top has the wool arranged a bit differently. I have used primarily four different colors, adding nickel-sized dots scattered over the strips of wool. Try these slippers, they are really easy to make! You may just need to first adjust the size of the slipper base, the sole, and the slipper top. I have provided two pattern pieces in two sizes but as I mentioned above you may need to adjust these as I am sure you do not have big old wide feet like me. But after all, these are scuff style slippers - not fitted shoes.

Fabric requirements

Army blanket or other thick wool 10" x 12" base for slipper top

Old blue green wool 5" x 6" for slipper top, dots

Pea green wool 5" x 6" for slipper top, dots

Brown wool 5" x 6" for slipper tops, dots

Army green wool 5" x 6" for slipper top, dots

Old blue green wool 1" x 9" for trim, slipper top

Army green wool 1" x 9" for trim, slipper top

Old black wool 10" x 11" for slipper sole top

Army blanket or other thick wool 10" x 11" for slipper sole bottom

Army blanket or other thick wool 20" x 11" for inner layer of sole

Chipboard such as cereal or cracker box 20" x 11" to stiffen slipper sole

Old black wool 1" x 28" for each slipper as binding

Coats and Clark thread summer brown

Hand sewing supplies

Glue stick

Cutting/Assembly

Begin by making your patterns. You can use the ones provided - if they do not fit, draw around one foot. (I suggest you wear a sock it will make it easier.) Flip the pattern over for your other foot. Add 1/4" all around (the inner sole for wools and cardboard are 1/4" smaller all around). Be sure to mark L and R so as not to get the slippers mixed up later. Mark the 3 guide marks on the slipper as well as the top mark on the top. The slipper opening along the top edges meets up with marks midway down the sole.

Slipper sole

Once you have your slipper sized, cut 2 - 1 each L and R of old black wool. Do the same out of Army blanket or other thick wool - cut 2 each L and R for the inner sole as well as 1 each of cardboard. I used the glue stick to lightly tack the inner sole wool to each side of the cardboard inner sole. Stack the Army blanket wool sole (bottom) then the inner sole wool, cardboard, inner sole wool then the old black wool sole on top. Stitch with a whip stitch all around the sole (see diagram A on page 39). You may want to use double thread here. Now make a second sole - be sure you have a left and right sole!

Slipper top

For the slipper top, I suggest you make a test piece and see how it fits when pinned to the sole. You want room for your toes but not so much you will lose your slipper. Cut out an Army blanket slipper top for each slipper. Use dyed wools to cover the slipper top. Stitch the wool in place in strips, trim away any excess. Make 6 assorted nickel-sized dots for each slipper and arrange on the slipper tops, mixing up the colors as you wish. See diagram B. For each slipper top, take a 1" x 9" wool strip and cut it into a pointy edging, then stitch across the top edge of the slipper. See diagram C. Line up the marks from the patterns, pin the top to the slipper base. Whip stitch using a double thread.

Finish

To finish the slippers, cut a strip of old black wool 1" x 28" for each slipper. Begin along the side of the slipper overlapping the top of assembled slipper by 1/4" and stitch the binding in place, covering the stitched edge of your slippers. Be sure half the strip is on the top. Stitching all around, flip over the slipper and stitch around the bottom edge. See diagram D.

That is really all there is to do. Take it a step at a time and you will have cozy, comfortable toe warmers to wear.

Note: I have thought about ways to make these non-slippery on polished floors, something I do not have to worry about with my old wood floors. One way is to use chamois cloth from the car section of the department stores and make the bottom soles from this. I have not tried it and since these are really just to warm your toes and not for running around the house, it might not be necessary.

I would not suggest these for little children as the loose fit may cause them to stumble.

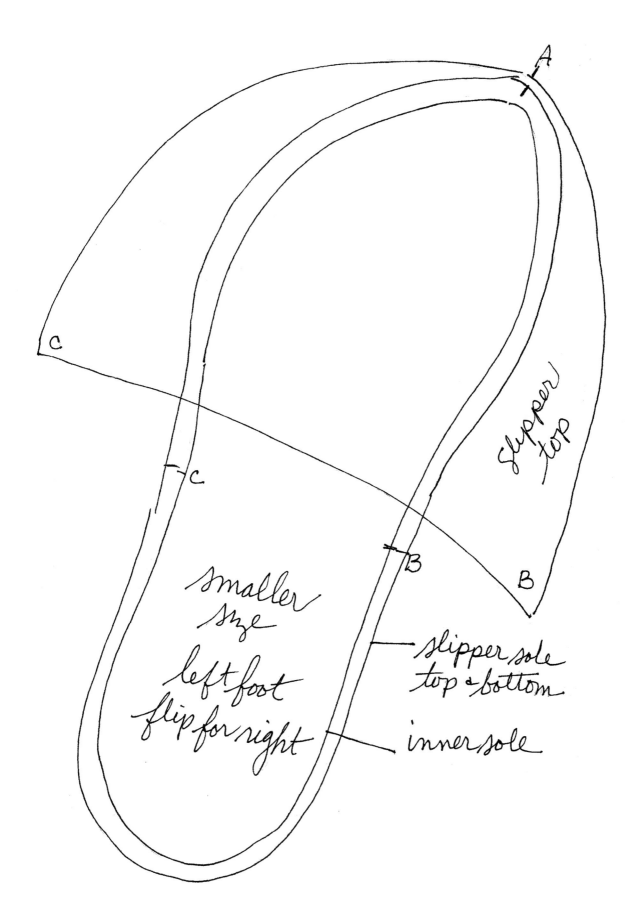

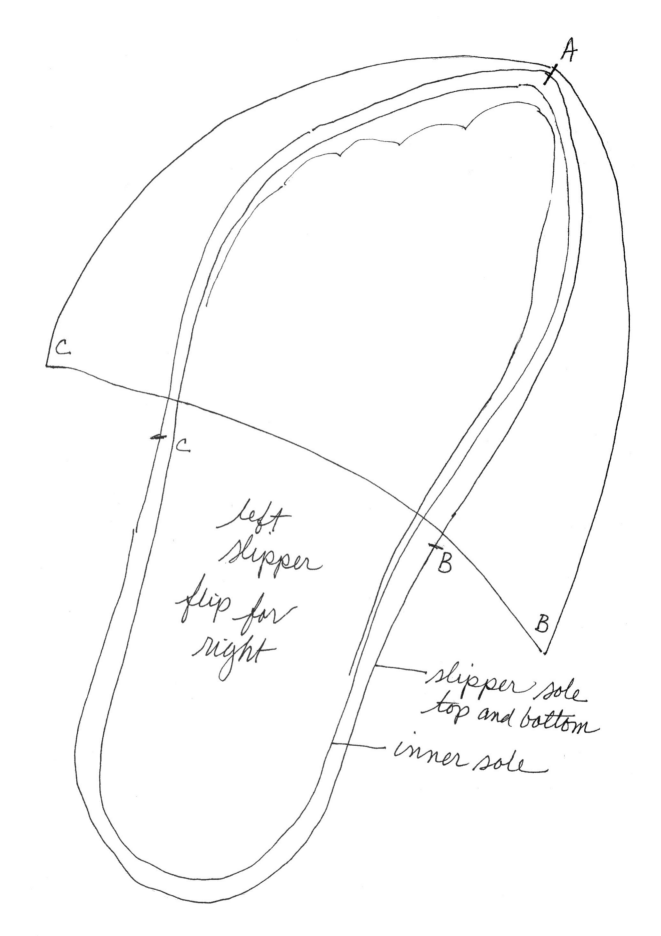

Diagram A

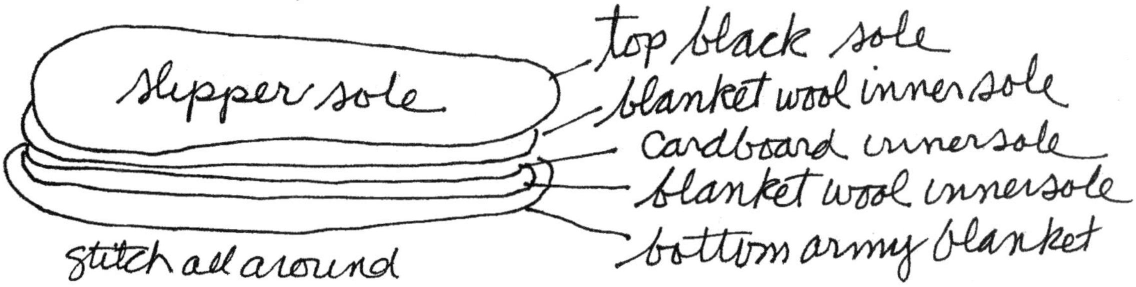

slipper sole

- top black sole
- blanket wool innersole
- cardboard innersole
- blanket wool innersole
- bottom army blanket

stitch all around

Diagram B
slipper top layout

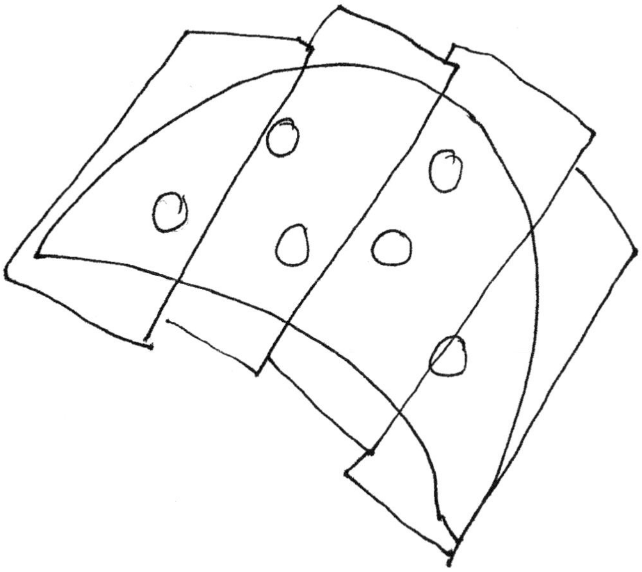

add wool trim

Diagram D.
stitch binding

slipper bottom

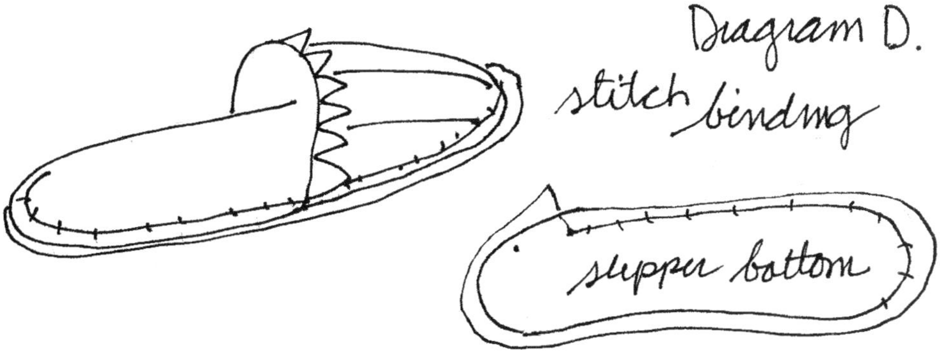

Simplify

Wool Mat

16" x 32"

Our life is frittered away by detail.
Simplify, simplify
— Thoreau

Great words, but simplifying is something I usually fail to do. I like "stuff". This mat is made from an old Army blanket. Now I don't crochet but must have picked up some crochet cotton somewhere, so I used it to blanket stitch around the lambs tongues. This worked for me and was more economical than purchasing floss or perle cotton. So the materials for this project were actually "simple" - a good reminder to me of what to strive for.

Fabric requirements and supplies

1 Army blanket or 1 yard of Army green/browny green wool
Antique white wool 9" x 11" for letters
Off-white crochet cotton: 52 yards for blanket stitched edging
Cotton homespun 9 1/2" x 25" for backing
Coats and Clark summer brown thread
Hand sewing supplies

Cutting/Assembly

Cut out a 24" x 9 1/2" rectangle from the Army blanket, then cut out a 21" x 8 1/2" rectangle. Cut out the letters from antique white wool, cut out the tongues from the Army blanket according to the pattern piece instructions.

Blanket stitch around all the tongues but do not stitch along the bottom edge. See the diagram on page 45.

Take the larger rectangle and pin 9 tongues behind the wool edges on the long sides and 3 tongues on the short sides. Add one tongue at each corner so they are behind the other

ongues (see photo). There may be spaces between the tongues. Stitch in place.

ake the smaller rectangle and arrange, hen appliqué the word "simplify" as in the hoto. Pin 8 tongues 1/2" behind long sides nd 2 tongues on each short side. Add one ongue on each corner. There may be space between the tongues. Stitch in place. Set the smaller rectangle on top of larger rectangle. Center, pin and carefully stitch to attach it to the back rectangle. You may have to lift the tongues as you stitch to secure the top piece. Add the backing by turning it under 1/2" all around, covering all the tongue ends with the cotton homespun. Stitch in place.

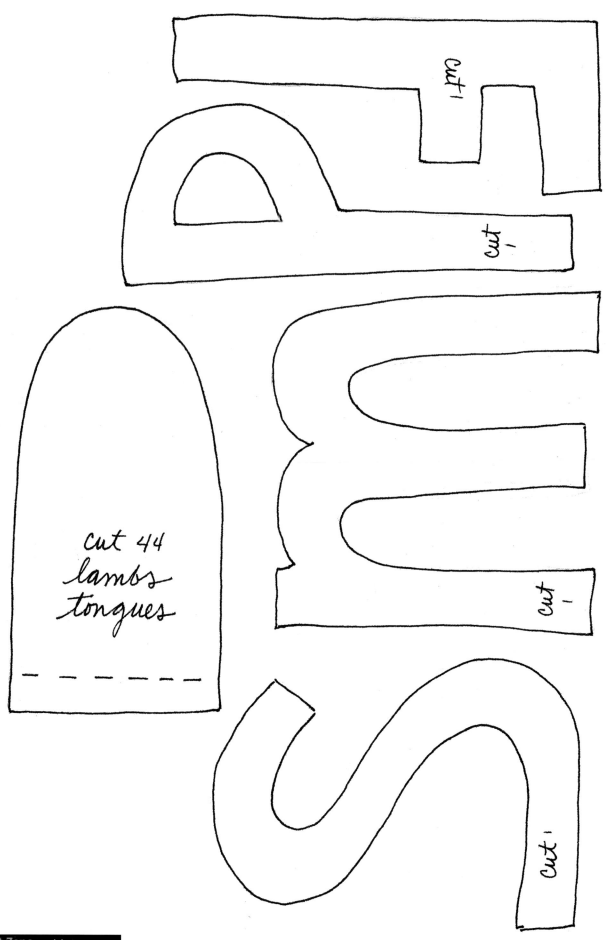

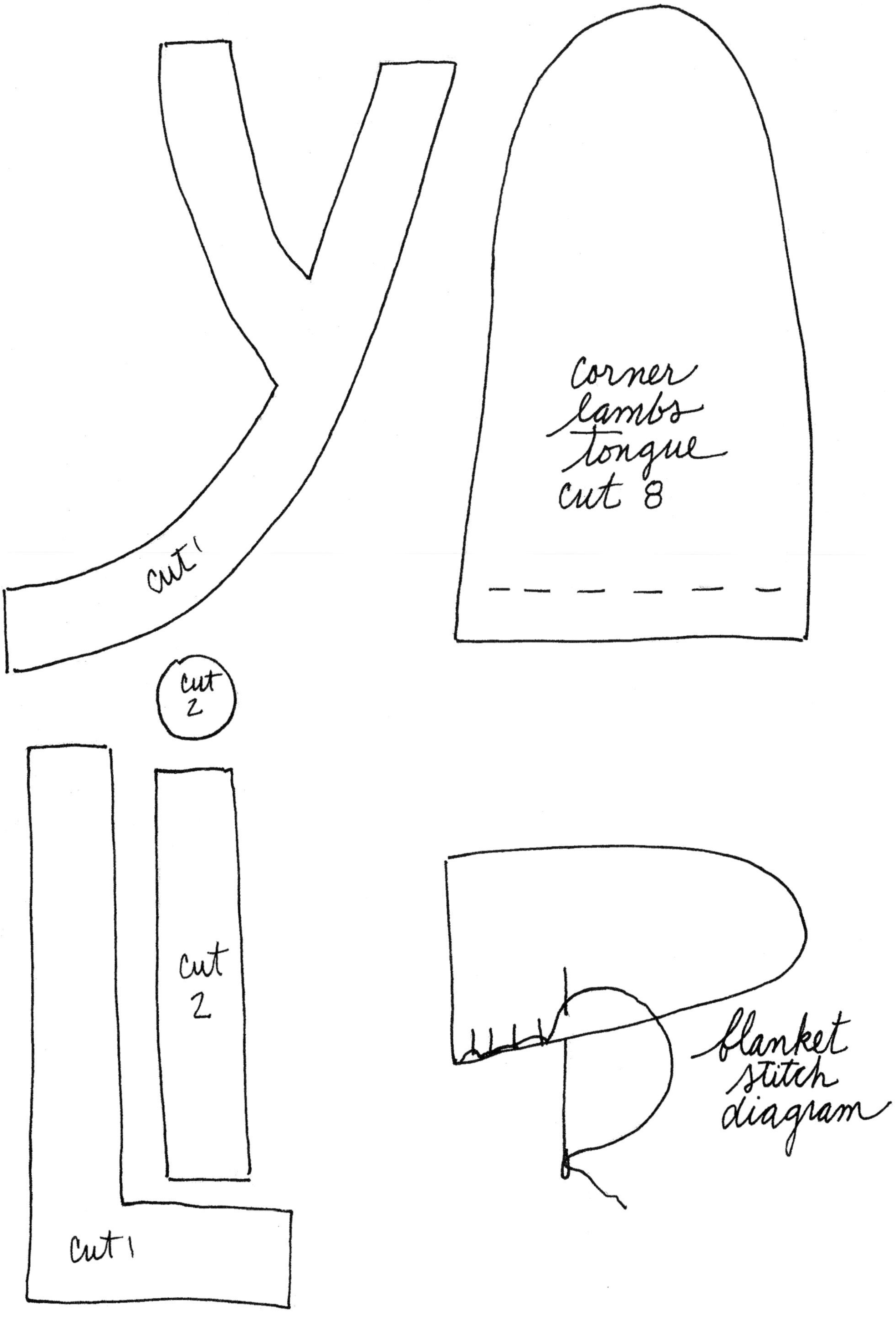

cut 1

corner lambs tongue cut 8

cut 2

cut 2

cut 1

blanket stitch diagram

> O Bed! O Bed!
> Delicious Bed!
> That heaven
> upon earth to
> the weary head
>
> MB

O Bed! O Bed! Wool Bed Cover

63" x 71"

O Bed! O Bed! Delicious Bed! That heaven upon earth to the weary head. -Thomas Hood

When you're tired, isn't that the way you feel about your bed? Nothing is more comforting than to sink down into your comfy bed and get some much needed sleep. Years ago I came across the little verse and always liked it. I knew when I began to work on this book it would be exactly what I wanted for a project with appliquéd words. I am grateful that someone else has a way to put words together that inspires me to stitch.

The overall color combination to this wool bed cover is subtle. The background uses various similar colored wools pieced randomly together into bands. The letters are cut from wool of varied colors, lighter than the background, but nothing that jumps out at you. I think it is a very calm and relaxing bed cover to crawl under for a nap! The border is also pieced together and there are a few lambs tongues scattered to add a little interest but not distract from the words. I think what works so well is the subtleness in the overall finished piece. Look for wools in closely related and hand dyed colors so there are lighter and darker areas - more color variation.

Fabric requirements and supplies

Dark colored wools for bed cover totaling approximately 4 yards using the following colors:

Old black
Dark smoky gray
Black brown plaid
Browny green light (green with brown tones)
Browny green dark (green with brown tones)
Brown
Spruce green
Blue green
Rust

Medium color wools for the letters and lambs tongues using the following colors, about 8" x 10" for each:

Greeny blue (blue with green tones)
Taupe
Light smoke gray
Light browny green (green with brown tones)
Blue green
Rust
Straw
Faded old black
Charcoal
Browny green (green with brown)
Faded blue green

Cotton homespun: 4 yards for backing (I used the leftover to back the Sleep Pillow Cover, page 54)
Coats and Clark summer brown sewing thread
Hand sewing supplies
Ruler/quilter's rule

Cutting/Assembly

Top

I first tore some of my assorted wools into 6" widths and randomly stitched them together to create a band 65" long. I overlapped the 6" edge about 1/4" and stitched together. For example, for one band I stitched together old black, browny green, brown then again browny green. Do not make the pieces the same length - you want them to be random. Another band may be old black, blue green, browny green, brown, black/brown plaid then more browny green. The 6" wide bands are the ones you will appliqué your letters to. When I planned out my words I did not cut out all of them ahead of time. I looked at the wool where the letter was to go and decided what color wool I would use. I did make all the letter bands as in the photo. There are 5 of these. Then I went back and pieced the blank bands - there are 4 of these. These are made the same way but are 7" wide. The bands with the words are placed so they overlap the plain ones by 1/2" all along the length of the band.

Borders

Once you have the 9 bands assembled and stitched together, make the borders. Make 2 bands 65" x 4 1/2" in the same random pieced manner. This will be attached along the top and bottom of the bed cover. Before attaching, piece together the 2 side borders 63" x 4 1/2" in the same way. Cut out an assortment of lambs tongues from the same wools as the letters. Leave some plain, make some with a second tongue on top or just one penny circle. Add them randomly - single or in groups - along the edge of your border bands. For example, I grouped 5 different tongues with one having a second tongue on it then down the band I grouped 3, then 2, then 4. The idea is to add a little color along the border but not have everything laid out exactly the same for each border. Use the photo as a guide. These tongues are placed along the edge that stitched to the bed cover center.

Backing

I backed this bed cover with a brown checked homespun, use what you wish. I had to join lengths of homespun, seamed down their length to become double wide. I laid the homespun face down and the bed cover right side up and pinned the layers together. I used the same thread and stitched along the bands where they join together to secure the backing to the front. Once done, I left about 1" all around the outer edge turning in the raw edge between the layers and just whip-stitched all around.

2 ea

2 ea

1 ea

1 ea

h, a, v,
r, u, w, p

4 ea

5 ea

1 ea

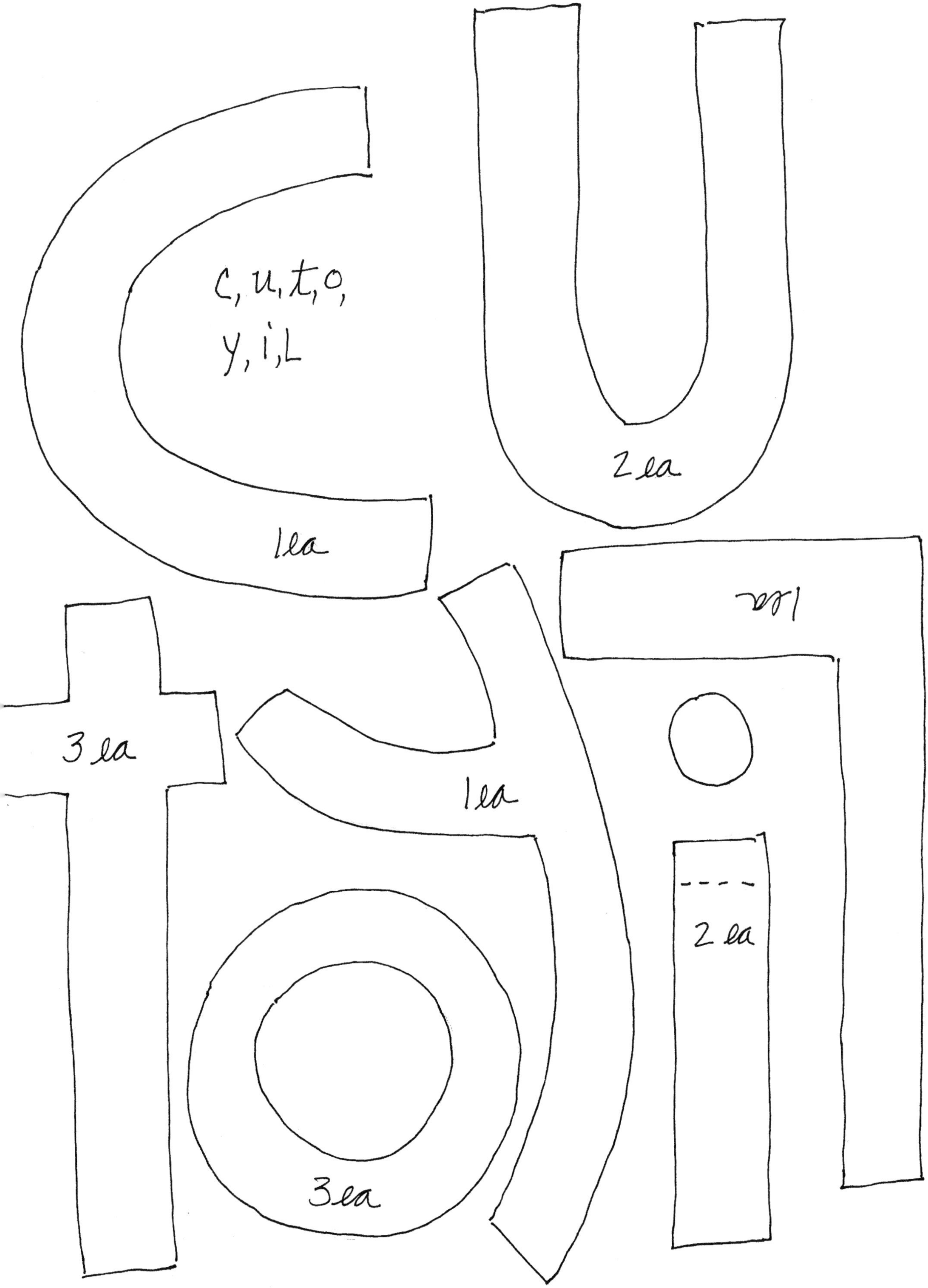

c, u, t, o, y, i, L

1 ea

2 ea

3 ea

1 ea

1 ea

2 ea

3 ea

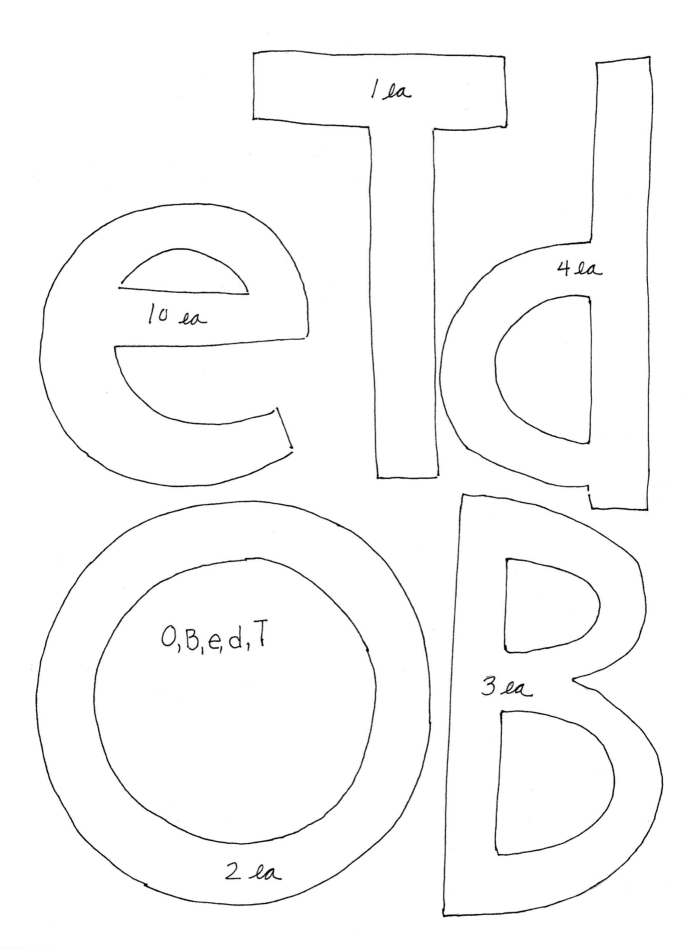

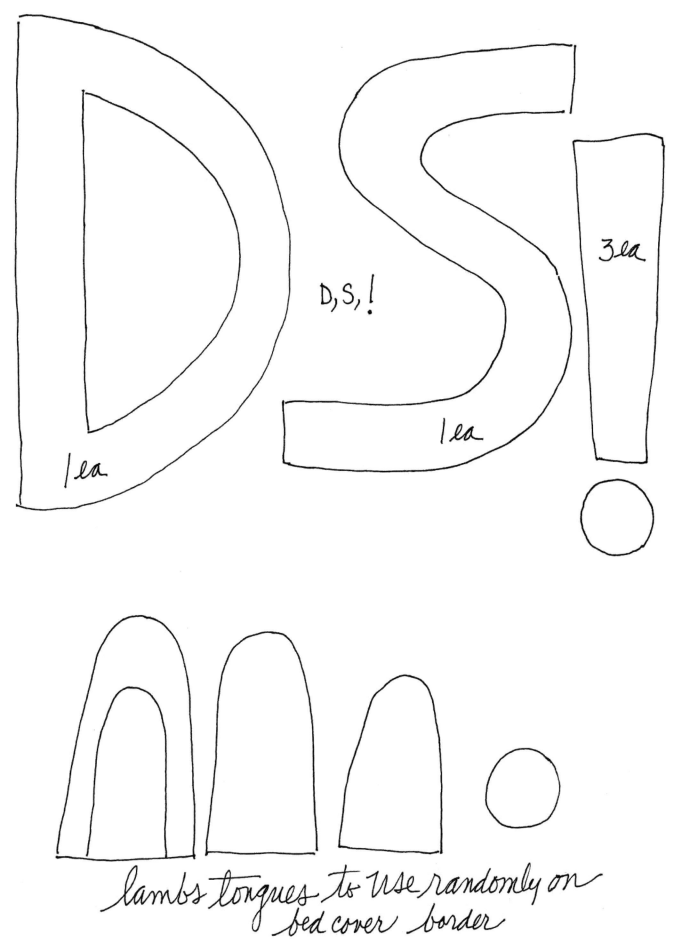

Comfort Zone 54

Sleep Pillow Cover

40 1/2" x 18 1/2"

Ahhh, sleep! There is nothing like it at the end of a busy day! This project was designed to go with the O Bed! Bed Cover. Again, I use wools that are closely related in color for the background, the darks as well as the appliquéd part, and some medium/light wools. I have drawn up a diagram to guide you (see page 57).

Fabric requirements and supplies

Chestnut brown (medium dark brown) wool 13 1/2" x 35 1/2" for mat background
D - old black 10" x 16" for border
B - light greeny brown wool 16" x 11" for leaves, border. S, e, p, z, berry
B-dk - dark greeny brown wool fat quarter for border, stems, lamb tongues, urn scallops
A - blue green wool 7" x 12" for urn, z, leaves, lamb tongues, berries
F - taupe wool 6" x 10" for leaves, e, lamb tongue
E - smoky gray wool 6" x 10" for z, leaves
C - rust wool 3" x 8" for l, leaves, lamb tongues
G - dark brown wool 3" x 12" for z, lamb tongues
H - med brown wool 3" square for border
Brown check homespun 41 1/2" x 19 1/2" for backing
Hand sewing supplies
Coats and Clark summer brown sewing thread

Cutting/Assembly

Begin with the appliqué on the 13 1/2" x 35 1/2" background wool. Cut out the urn from the blue green wool and cut stems from the dark browny green wool. The stem measurements are the numbers on the designated stems in the diagram, cut the length x 1/4". Once the stems are in place, cut out the remaining appliqué pieces - use the diagram for color information. Stitch all in place. Assemble the borders with random lengths of wool in 3" wide pieces. Use the diagram for color suggestions - be sure to make the wool in different lengths. Make 2 bands 35 1/2" long and 2 that are 18 1/2". Before attaching these borders, cut out the lamb tongue as suggested in the diagram. Use the pattern pieces, mix up the sizes and stitch in place.

Stitch the 2 long borders, then the 2 side borders. Lay borders 1/2" under the edge of mat, stitch in place.

Attach the backing, lay the homespun face down with the mat right side up, leaving 1/2" of the backing to turn in under the wool. Pin in place and stitch all around.

I want to be seen here in my simple, natural, ordinary fashion, without straining or artifice; for it is myself that I portray ... I am myself.

Montaigne
1533-1592

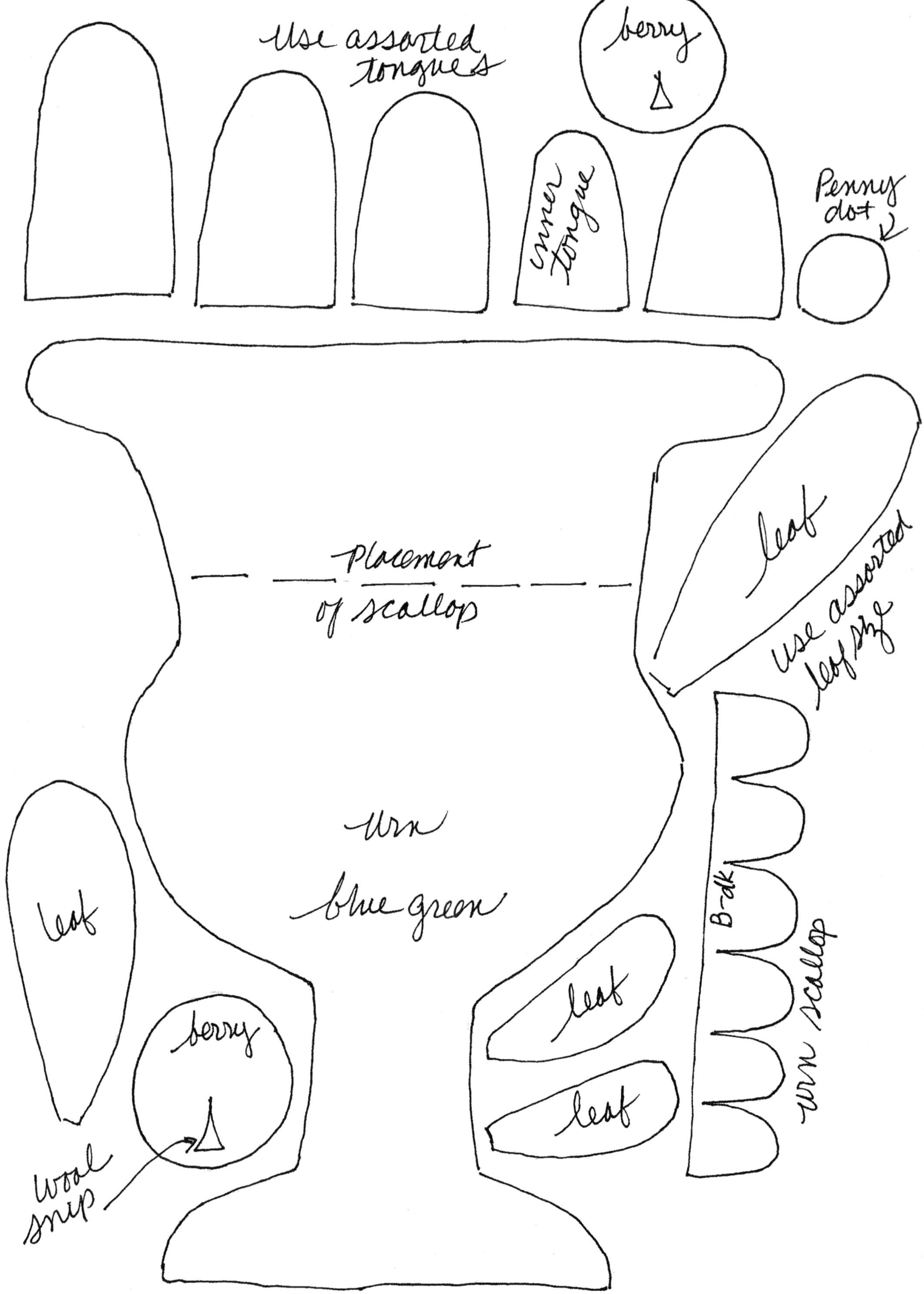

Use assorted tongues

berry

inner tongue

Penny dot

placement of scallop

leaf
Use assorted leaf sizes

Urn
blue green

leaf

B-dk

leaf

leaf

berry

wool snip

urn scallop

Urn Full of Flowers Appliquéd Mat

15" x 23"

This old black urn hosts a simple bunch of flowers waiting to be set in the middle of an old country table or on the mantle of your favorite room. They look a little like they would be found out in a field or along the road. My favorite found flowers have always been goldenrod. I fill a crock with huge bundles and put it in my house. The color is always wonderful (a little like the soft mustard color in this piece). And it always surprised me that people thought I was bringing in a great bunch of allergens. I never once sneezed!

This piece is wool appliqué on sand colored raw silk. Because it is pre washed, it has a nubby look and texture. I have left this unfinished but you could add a backing, make it into a pillow or even frame it. I like to be able to move it around - from pinning on a door to laying it on a chair back - just wherever it strikes my fancy.

Fabric requirements

Prewashed sand silk Matka (raw silk) 23" x 15" for background

Black wool 9" x 6" for urn

Old blue green wool 4" x 7" for large flower centers, berries

Rusty brown wool 3" x 8" for flower petals, flower fringe

Dark olive green wool 12" x 3" for stems, leaves, seeds, sprig

Pea green wool 5" x 6" for leaves, berries

Army green wool 11" x 4" for stems, leaves

Mustard wool 4" x 6" for urn scallop, seeds, berries, flowers

Coats and Clark summer brown thread

Hand sewing supplies

Walnut ink antiquing

Cutting/Assembly

Prepare the raw silk by antiquing it with the walnut dye, see page 11 for instructions. Once this is complete, refer to the photo and diagram on page 63 for layout. Cut 1/8" strips for stems, tuck the ends into the urn and under the flowers. Be sure the urn is centered and 1" above the bottom edge. Stitch everything in place and you are done.

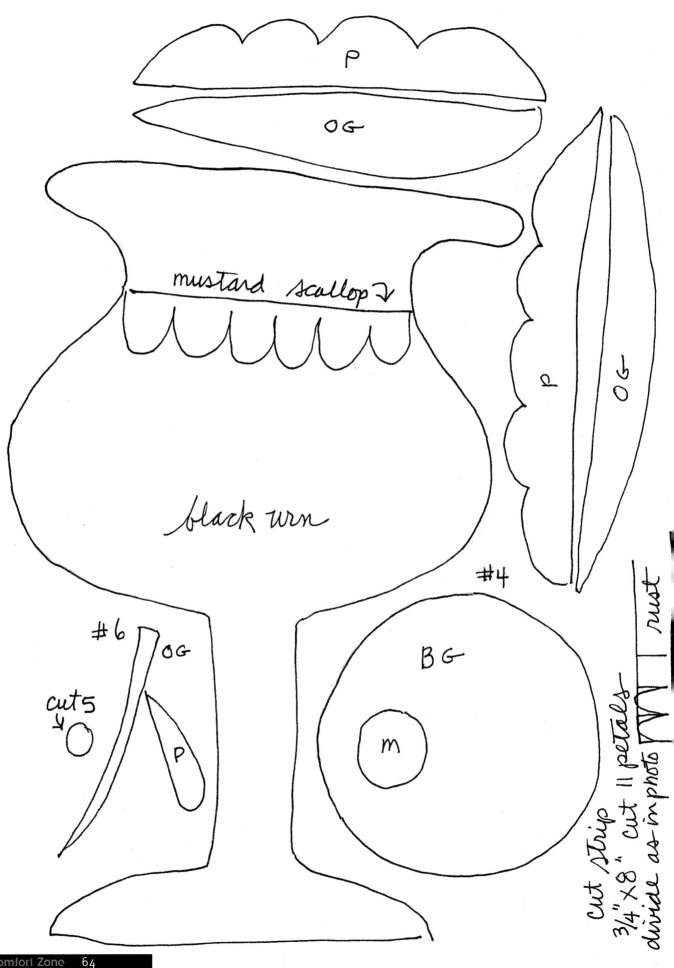

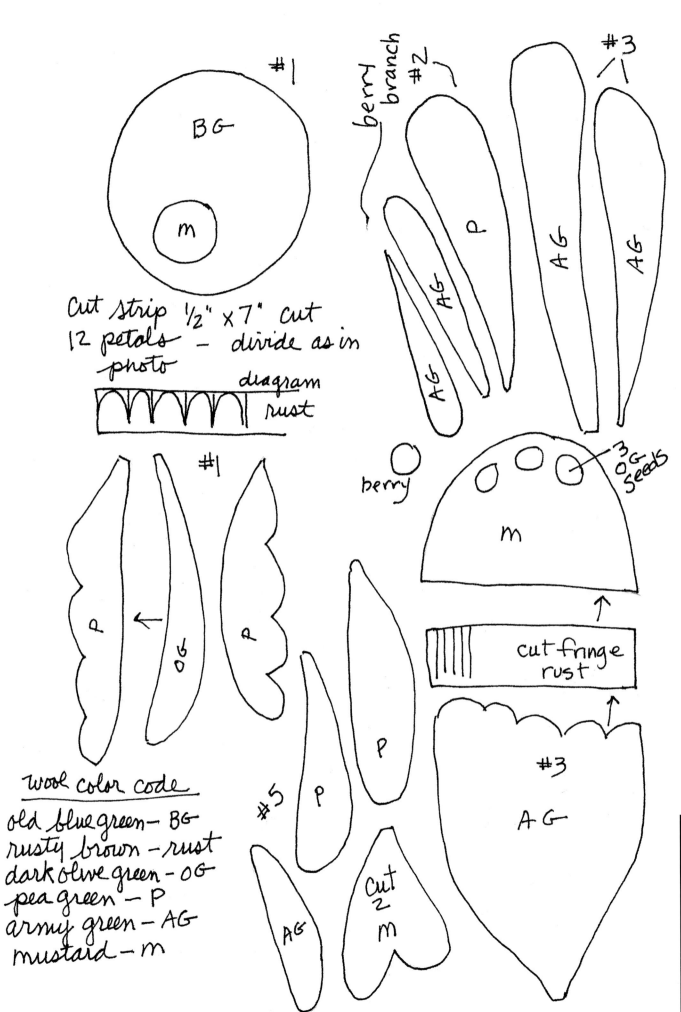

Black Wool Pomegranate Runner

10" x 44"

This project began when I did not have a piece of wool as long as I wanted, so I pieced together enough black wool to get the 44" length. I actually like it better than a solid piece. I wanted to keep the design simple and in dark colors. I think the Army green, rust and faded mustard look rich against the mixed blacks of the background. This vine - and I do know pomegranates do not grow on a vine, I actually saw them for the first time years ago visiting my Dad way down in Texas.... They were growing on a tree in the neighbors' yard. I was amazed and had to go over to take a photograph. Well back to the vine - and its leaves weaving slowly across the mat with three pomegranates and seeds.... well and of course your initials, you could add the year if you choose. You will also notice in the photo that I have left the edge of the wool irregular and I did not add any backing.

Fabric requirements and supplies

Black wool: enough to piece together a 10" x 44" runner while allowing at least a 1/4" overlap for stitching sections together

Army green wool 14" x 15" for leaf and vine

Rust wool 3" x 13" for pomegranates, initial

Faded mustard wool 3" square for seeds and initial

Coats and Clark summer brown thread

Hand sewing supplies

Cutting/Assembly

Piece together the black wool background. Make the vine by piecing together enough 1/2" green wool strip to make a 41" vine. Pin the vine in place. Cut out the leaves, pomegranates, seeds and initials – pin them in place using the photo as a guide. Stitch down using a simple whip stitch.

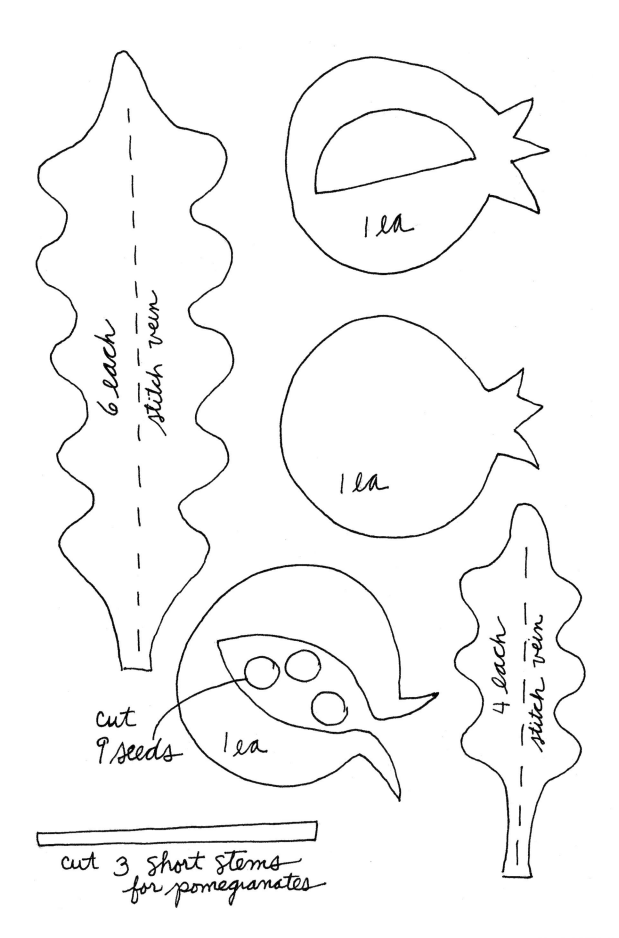

Red Wool Runner with Pomegranates

10" x 44"

This project is a result of being asked if I would ever do anything in bright colors, and this is bright for me! It is the same as the Black Wool Pomegranate Runner but with the volume turned up a bit. I have to say I had to step out of my comfort zone to even begin. I love the color combination. This was a lot of fun for me and a little like going from a photograph to a negative (we don't even have those any more with digital cameras). This project shows you can choose other colors if you prefer, just mind the fabric requirements when making your choices.

Fabric requirements and supplies

Tomato red wool in 3 different pieces: enough to make a 10" x 44" runner with enough extra to add the 1/4" overlaps to connect the pieces. You can use one piece if desired. I used plain red wool and one each small and tiny check weave.

Limey green wool: 2 different pieces totaling 14" x 15" for vine, leaves

Blue green wool 3" x 13" for pomegranate, initial

Yellow green wool 3" square for seeds and initial

Coats and Clark summer brown thread

Hand sewing supplies

Cutting/Assembly

Piece the red wool to make a 10" x 44" runner. Piece the vine together using 1/2" limey green wool strips stitched together to make a 41" vine. Refer to the photo to arrange the vine, pin. Cut out the remaining pieces - leaves, pomegranates, seeds and initials - place and pin. Stitch down. There is no backing.

Pins

A Useful Pincushion
8" x 4 1/2"

I do not think you can have too many pincushions. I love to make them and then line them up or group them together. Sometimes they are little works of art, sometimes little gifts of friendship or of a memory made of fabric that is special and reminds you of someone.

This pincushion falls into a little graphic design category as well as just being functional. The word "cushion" is a little misleading because this one is hard due to the birdcage grit that fills it....so it's not soft like a cushion, and how cushy is something that's filled with pins?? Just wondering.....

Fabric requirements and supplies

Black wool 10" x 8 1/2" for pincushion
Brown wool 5" x 3 1/2" for letters
Small bit of cotton stuffing (cotton balls could substitute here)
1 box parakeet/birdcage grit filler for pincushion
Coats and Clark summer brown thread
Hand sewing supplies

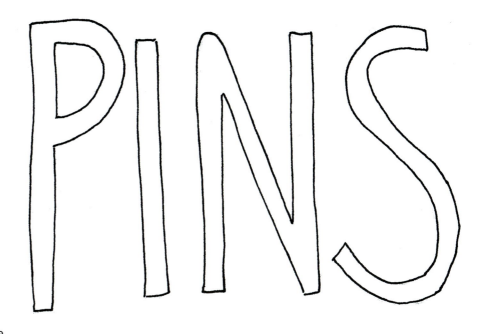

Cutting/Assembly

Cut the black wool into 2 - 5" x 8 1/2" pieces. Cut out the letters and appliqué them to one black wool rectangle. Lay the appliquéd side face down on the other piece of black wool, stitch around 3 sides. Turn right side out, fill the bottom corners with cotton, then fill with the grit, and top with more cotton stuffing. This should be firmly packed. Fold in the edges and stitch closed,

Add your pins and you are ready to go. This pincushion sits firmly in place keeping your pins handy. For a lesson in aging pin tops, see page 11.

Two Working Rollups

Stitching Rollup

Fabric requirements and supplies

Limey green wool 17" x 13" for outer layer, leaves, stem

Cotton flannel 17" x 11 1/2" for batting

Brown and cream stripe cotton fabric 18" x 12 1/2" for inside layer

Army green wool 10" x 16" for stems, leaves, flower centers, pocket, and rectangle for letters

Blue green wool 8" x 6" for flower centers, letters

Red wool 10" x 6" for flowers, pincushion

Limey green silk ribbon

Coats and Clark summer brown thread

Cotton stuffing

Cutting/Assembly

Cut out the limey green wool cover (17" x 11 1/2"). Cut wool strips from the Army green wool for the stems, cut one 12" x 1/2" for design center. Cut 3 - 4" x 1/8" for side flowers. Cut out the pattern using the information provided, arrange them using the photo as a guide. Pin in place and stitch down. Lay the cotton right side down, lay the flannel on top, turn down the 1/2" raw edge of the cotton fabric over the flannel. Lay the appliquéd cover on top, right side up and pin together. Fold up one end of the ribbon 15" and tuck the folded end between the wool and cotton layers, centered along the narrow end of the rollup by the red flower. Stitch all around to secure the layers and ribbon.

Use the photo as a guide to arrange the appliqué pieces on the striped fabric. Lay the rollup so the ribbon is on the left. Cut out the pocket from the Army green wool (6 1/4" x 4 1/2"). Appliqué a stem of limey green 1/4" x 6" to the center of the pocket, add leaves. Stitch the pocket in place 1" above bottom edge and 2" in from left side. Add the red flower with centers.

Add the red wool pincushion (cut 9 1/2" x 2 3/4") in the center area. Pin 3 sides down, then add stuffing and finish pinning, stitch in place. Cut out a rectangle of Army green wool 8 3/4" x 4 1/2". Place it 1" in from the right side, centered on the cotton, and stitch down, Cut out the letters and appliqué them to the green rectangle.

Now add sewing necessities, roll up and get ready to stitch.

Wool Hooking Rollup
17" x 11 1/2"

This project combines two of my favorite pastimes - hooking and stitching. My favorite wools combine to make a useful roll up to store and carry my hooking necessities. And it's easy to tote along with me to rug hooking class.

This project makes using up bits of your favorite wool easy!

Fabric requirement for cover

Dark brown wool, 17" x 4 1/4" for cover
Old black 17" x 3" for cover
Browny green 17" x 5" for cover
Army green wool 16" x 2" for vine, leaves, flower base
Old straw wool 2" x 3" for flower
Rust wool 2" x 4" for initial
Old blue green 3" x 4" for initial
1/2" wide black twill tape for 1 yard tie

Comfort Zone

Fabric requirements for inside

Browny green wool 17" x 11 1/2" for inside
Fabric for pieced pocket:
    Old black wool 3" x 9"
    Browny green wool 2 1/2" x 8"
    Light browny green 2 1/2" x 8"
    Dark brown wool 2 1/2" x 6 1/2"
    Dark spruce green 2 1/2" square
    Old blue green 2" x 3" for patch

Fabric requirements for letters

Old blue green wool 4" x 3" for h, o
Dark brown wool 2" square for o
Old black wool 2" x 4" for k
Faded straw wool 1/2" x 3" for i
Medium brown wool 2" x 2 1/2" for n
Dark browny green 4 1/2" x 2" for g
2 - 3/4" shell buttons
Coats and Clark summer brown thread

Assembly - cover

Stitch the 3 cover wools (dark brown, old black and browny green) to make the cover (17" x 11 1/2"), with the old black wool in the center overlapping the other 2 pieces. Cut the vine to 16" x 1/4", then cut the leaves and flower base, as well as flower. Refer to the photo to arrange the pieces, stitch in place. Add initials. Fold the twill tape in half, pin along right side at center, stitch.

Assembly - inside

Cut the pocket top band 1" x 9" from old black wool. Cut one pocket band from old black wool 5 1/2" x 2 1/4". Piece together the browny green, light browny green, dark brown and dark spruce wool pieces to make the pocket (9" x 8") with the old black wool band across the top. Refer to the photo as a guide. Add the old blue green patch, then make buttonholes in the top band of the pocket, 2 1/2" in from each side. Place the pocket 3/4" above the bottom edge, 1" in from left side, stitch. Sew on the 2 buttons for the pockets. Cut out the letters and sew them along the right edge of the rollup.

Layer the cover (right side down with the twill tape on the left) atop the inside piece (face up with pocket at left). Pin the 2 layers together, stitch all around.

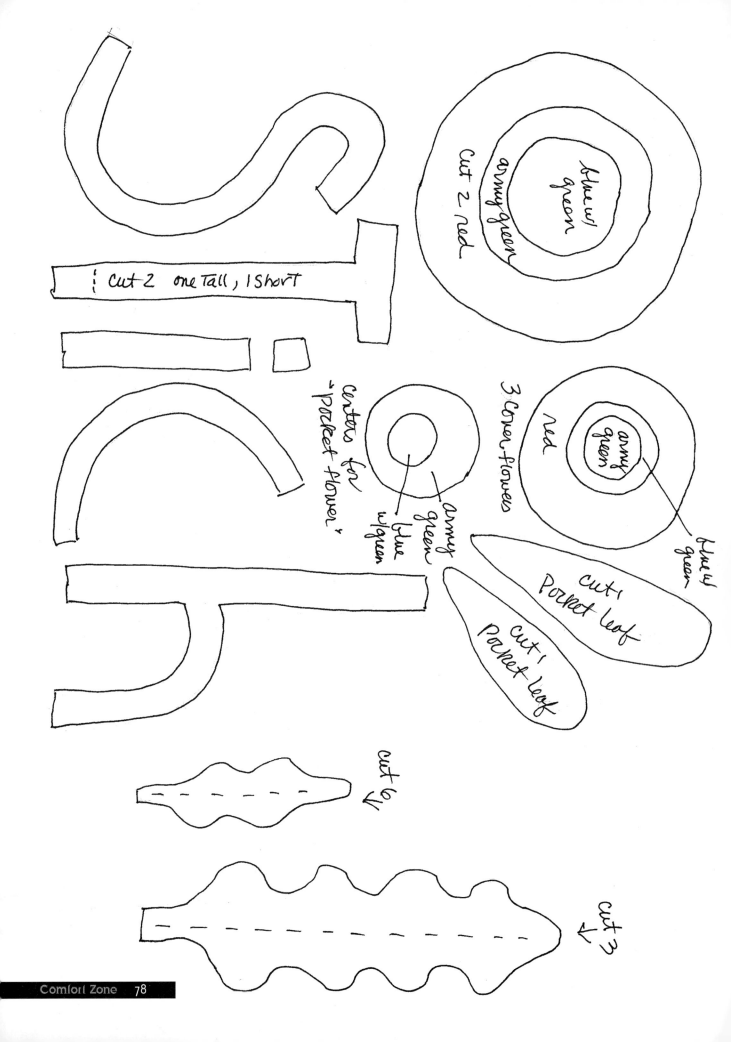

Crazy Wool Jacket

This is a wonderfully comfortable non-structured jacket. By this I mean it is loose fitting, with no darts or set-in sleeves, no tailoring. I would describe it as a kimono style with drop shoulders and sleeves rolled up at the wrists. I used different color wools for each of the different parts of the jacket. As I designed this jacket, I was actually looking for a way to make something warm that I could wear - not just cover up with - as well as use some of my favorite wools. This is another place where necessity is the mother of invention! We were in the middle of one of our longest, coldest and snowiest winters and as much as I love my old house, it is without any insulation, and it was cold this year. This project could be made up of other fabrics if you do not require cozy wools to keep you warm.

I must say this project made me move way out of my comfort zone as far as a wearable goes and color as well but the result is just perfect!

After I made my jacket, I asked my friend Michelle if I could use her as a manikin to make another model. I told her she would have to lay on the floor on top of some newsprint and I would draw around her, just like we used to do to make doll clothes! She is such a good friend she said she would do it but I am sure she was much relieved that was not the case. I came to her office with an armload of wool. I measured her and tore wool and began to pin. Then I went home and basted together the main body of the jacket for her to try on. I recommend that you do some pinning and basting so you find the fit that you like.

Fabric requirements and supplies

These will vary because of each person's size. I think we used between 2 1/2 and 3 yards of assorted wools total. My jacket has 8 different wools; Michelle's has 9 different wools. Wools that are 'off the bolt' need to be pre washed.

Tape measure

Hand sewing supplies (I stitched my jacket by hand and recommend that but if you prefer, use a sewing machine)

Thread: I used my favorite - Coats and Clark summer brown - but use what you prefer

2 small shell buttons for the cat appliqué

Perle cotton for whiskers on cat

Cutting/Assembly Jacket

Use a 1/2" seam allowance. My examples are given for Michelle's jacket, a medium size 10-12, and my jacket, which is extra large. Take this in steps - the measurements you take will help you decide how much wool you will need.

Front/Back: Measure Length and Width

First, with your arms down at your side measure from the top of the shoulder down your front to your fingertips. Now subtract 4 to 4 1/2" (this will be added back later in the band on the bottom edge of the jacket). Measure across the back of your hips from side seam to side seam. This is now the length and width of your jacket back. Cut the jacket back using this measurement. For the front use the same measurement - divide in two so you have a left and right front piece. Stitch the shoulder seams, leaving 11" in the center open for neckline, adjust as needed. Mark sides for armholes by measuring up from bottom edge of side seam 12"-14", mark this with a pin. See diagram A on page 84.

Sleeves

Sleeve measurement: from the drop shoulder line (edge of wool) to about mid hand (see diagram B) will give your sleeve length and this will allow for a rolled cuff. The measurement from the mark (see diagram A), for the armhole to the shoulder will be doubled - that will become your sleeve width. One of my sleeves was one piece of wool, one had three pieces of wool stitched together to give me the needed amount. On Michelle's jacket the sleeves are each made from 2 different wools. See diagram B.

Side panel

Before you can attach the sleeves you need to add a side panel and a gusset for the sleeve. To do this use the measurement you took from the bottom edge of the jacket to the 'armhole'. Depending on your jacket size, make a panel that length by 2 1/2"-4" wide.

Gusset

You can use pattern for the gusset on page 85 and adjust the size - it will need to be as wide as the side panel you just made. See diagram C on page 85. Attach the gusset to this side panel. Now sew the side panels to the front and back pieces of your jacket and sew on sleeves. You will want to taper the underarm seam for your sleeve towards wrist. See diagram D, page 86. Now you have the basic structure done.

Bottom edge panels

For this band, I made 4 1/2" or 5" long bands x the same widths as the jacket back and fronts of assorted wools. Stitch these together randomly, overlapping edges and whip stitching together to fit the bottom edge of your jacket. You may add some lambs tongues or pennies or vertical patches as you wish. When complete, attach it to the jacket body, overlapping the jacket by 1/2", whip stitch it in place. See diagram E. Make another band to face this band inside your jacket, stitch in place. Now topstitch, catching the seam overlap along edge where band attached to jacket body; see diagram F.

Facing

To face the front edge of the jacket, add 5 1/2" wide bands of wool down the length of jacket front, piece these as you wish, whip stitch down front opening. I added an appliqué of a cat face in honor of Michelle's sweet kitty Kiki on the inside of her jacket's front facing.

Back neck facing is applied on the outside as another design element with a rectangle of contrasting wool as another bit of color. See diagram G and pattern guide.

Pockets

The pockets are 7 1/2" or 8 1/2" square. Trim with a 1 1/2" piece of contrasting wool the length of the pocket side. Stitch half to the outside of the pocket, fold over and stitch other half on inside of pocket. Pockets are placed on the jacket front 1-1 1/2" above the lower band and 2 1/2"-3" in from the front edge of the jacket. Pin and see if you like the placement - if so, stitch in place. See diagram H.

You have a completed jacket, a blank canvas. Add some appliqué if desired, find a great button if you want for a jacket closure, attach some twill as ties or add a heart or turnip pin.

This is your crazy wool jacket, do as you wish.

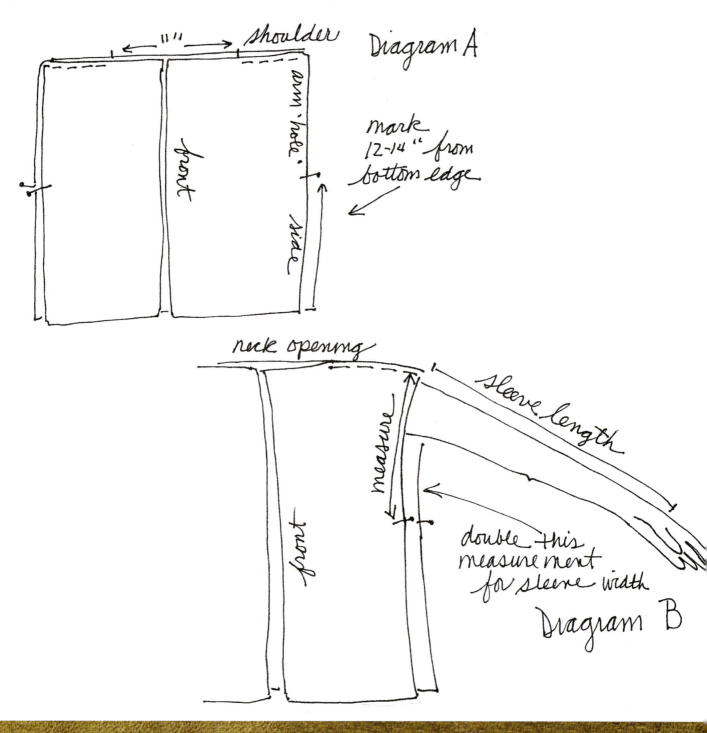

gusset pattern
xlg + med

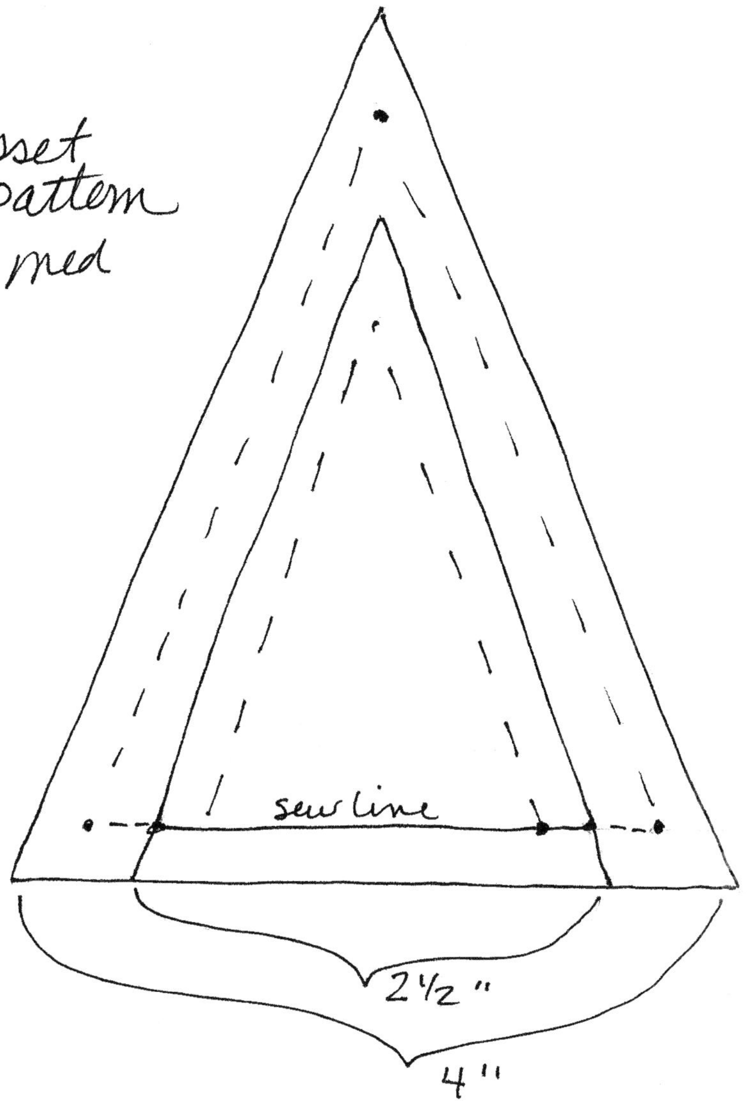

sew line

2½"

4"

shoulder

Diagram C

jacket side

12"-14" by 2½" or 4" side panel

sew gusset to side panel

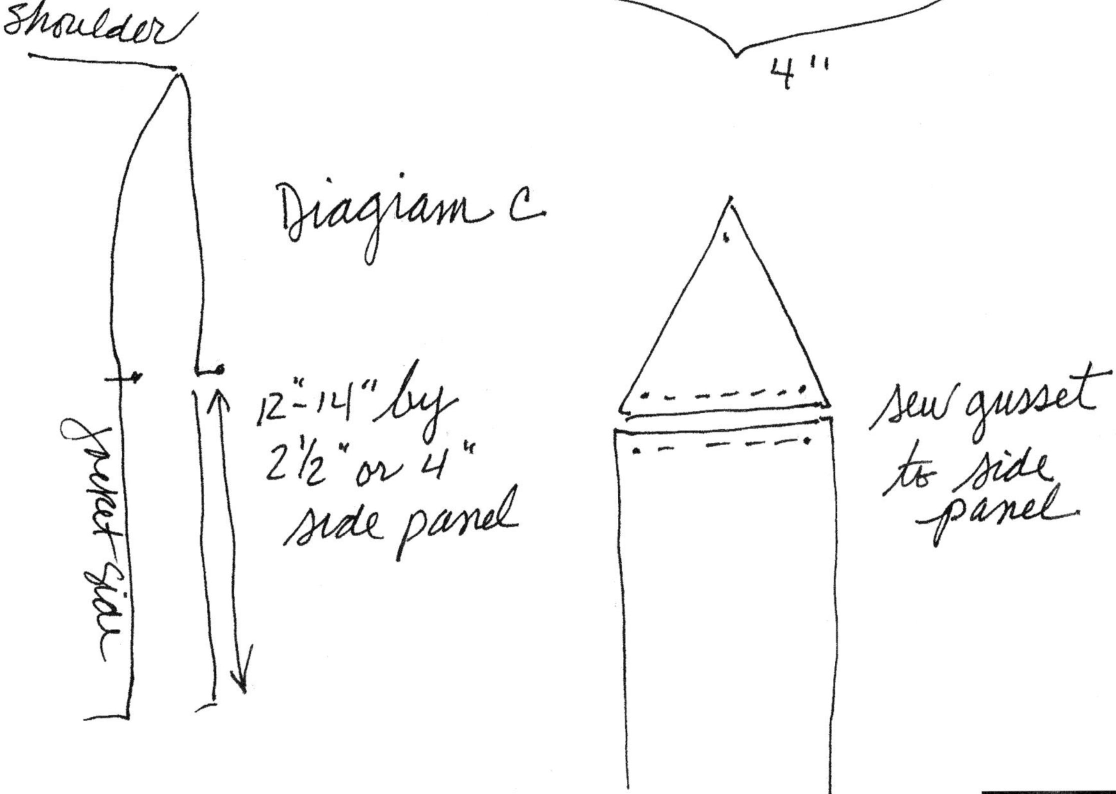

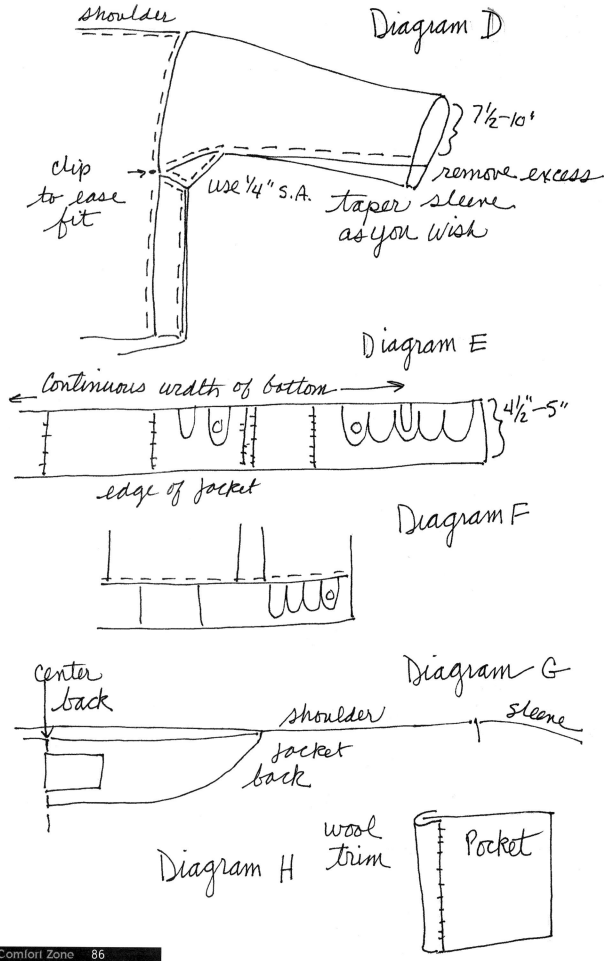

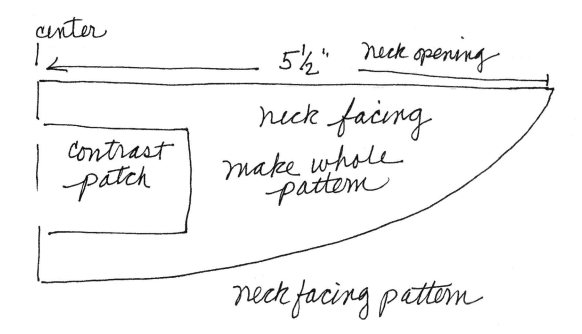

neck facing pattern

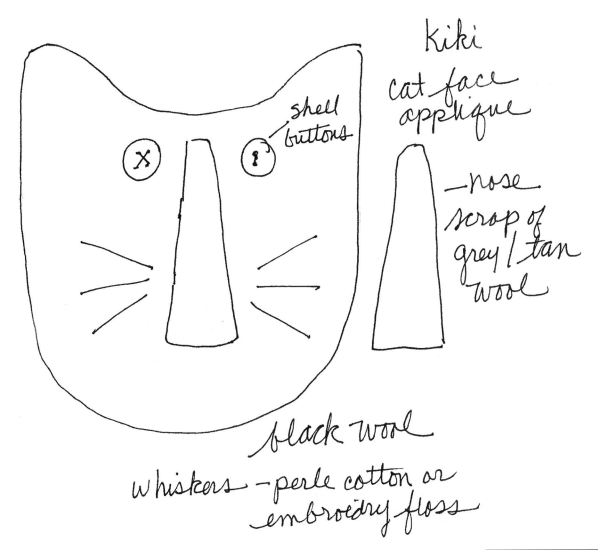

Heart Pin

Here's a little something to make and wear on your crazy wool jacket. I have used red velvet but any fabric could work just as well.

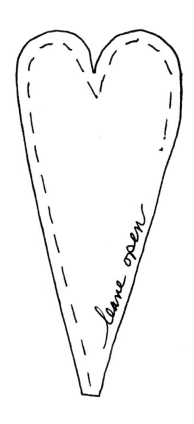

Fabric requirements and supplies

Cotton velvet or fabric of your choice
4" x 5" for the heart

Cotton stuffing

Thread

Hand sewing supplies

Cutting/Assembly

Cut out 2 hearts with right sides together stitch as shown on pattern. Clip curves and the 'v', turn and stuff, stitch closed. I use a safety pin to attach it to clothing.

Turnip Pin

I have been asked to give the pattern for my turnip pin. The crazy wool jacket is the perfect place to wear it, so here it is. I used cotton fabric available in shops.

Fabric requirements

Plum/purple cotton calico or plain 8" x 4" for turnip

Bronzy green cotton print or plain 4" x 5" for turnip leaves

Dark tan cotton 4" x 5" for turnip leaves* or double the bronzy green cotton instead

4" x 5" fusible web

Thread

Tacky glue

One fiber covered floral wire - 15" of 32 gauge wire

Hand sewing supplies

Iron

Cutting/Assembly

Cut out the turnip following the pattern: note it is cut on the bias. With right sides together, sew as shown on pattern. Turn right side out, stuff partially and stitch up the skinny root, turning in the raw edge as you stitch.

Prepare 3 leaves as directed in diagram, using the pattern for the leaf. Use the paper leaf pattern to mark the leaves, lining up the fused floral wire to the leaf stem, see diagram.

Make a running stitch along the top edge of the turnip to draw it closed, add stuffing as you go. Before drawing it completely closed, put a few drops of glue down the center. Insert the ends of the 3 leaves, then pull it closed securing the leaves; knot off.

Comfort Zone

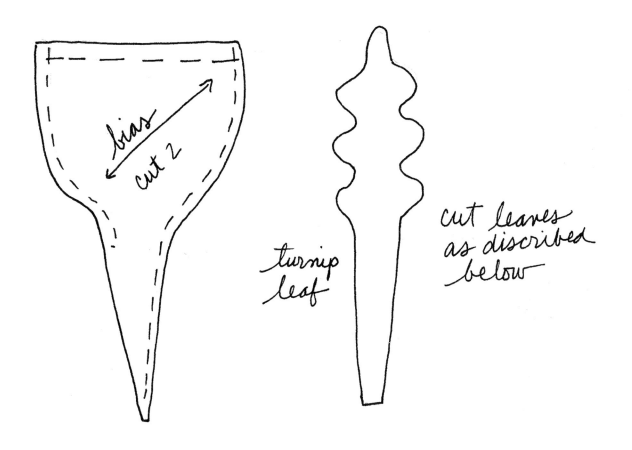

turnip leaf

cut leaves as discribed below

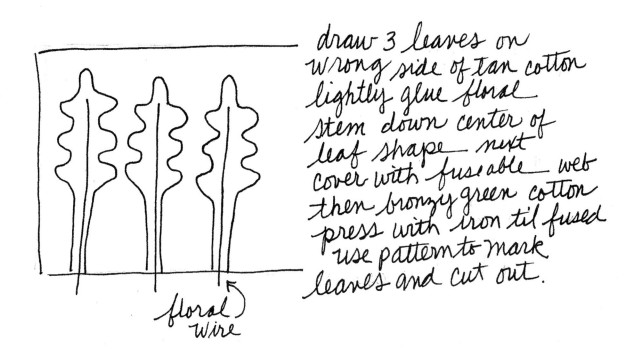

floral wire

draw 3 leaves on wrong side of tan cotton lightly glue floral stem down center of leaf shape next cover with fuseable web then bronzy green cotton press with iron til fused use pattern to mark leaves and cut out.

Colored Blocks Hooked Rug

24" x 42"

This hooked rug was made as a utility rug to use up a lot of assorted dark wool and some thrift store clothing. I like the way this rug looks with both scraps and old clothing. When I made it I was still using a size 6 cutter and because of the way the block is filled, I think a narrow cut will work best.

You can make this rug any size by hooking as many 6" blocks

Fabric requirements and supplies

Note: the amounts needed will vary slightly because of the height and density of your loops.
- Monks cloth or linen 32" x 50" for rug foundation
- Assorted black wool 1 1/2 yards
- Assorted mustard wool 1/2 yard
- Assorted blue wool 1/2 yard
- Assorted antique whites 1/2 yard
- Assorted gray wool 1/6 yard
- Sharpie marker
- Ruler
- Hooking supplies

Cutting/Assembly

Use a ruler and make 6" squares - draw 7 blocks across and 7 down. When you hook these blocks, use the directional marks drawn in the diagram. As you hook you will get a swirled pattern.

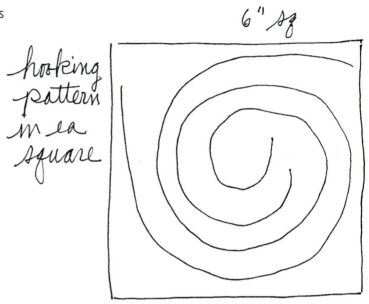

hooking pattern in ea square — 6" sq

Comfort Zone

Comfort Zone

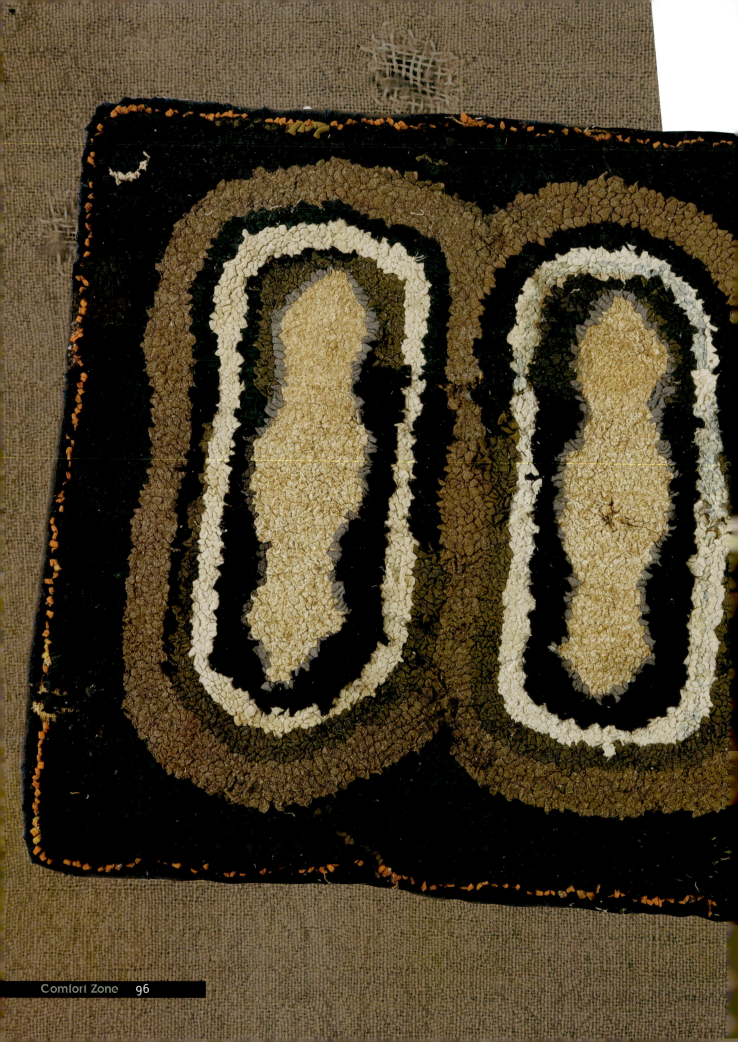

Primitive Ovals Hooked Rug

29" x 31"

This is inspired by an antique rug I bought that was in bad condition. The backing was burlap and had disintegrated quite a bit. I used monks cloth and used a wide cut strip so when I was done my rug did not have straight sides - I now know I need to use linen with my wide strips. I used my variation of colors and love the outcome but because I was careful to have my loops all even and straight, the rug lost some of the whimsy the antique rug had. I am not saying be careless with your hooking but there are some places where the less perfect hooking will add to the appeal of the finished rug. I used this method of just pulling up my loops willy-nilly, leaving the loops at varied heights and leaving any twists as they appear for my hooked rug Square in a Square (see page 107) which I made after this rug. You might try this technique sometime, maybe on a chair pad or seat cushion.

Fabric requirements and supplies

Note: these amounts will vary according to individual hooking style.

Linen foundation for wide cuts, Monks cloth for narrower cuts 37" x 38"

Assorted wools totaling about 3 yards (described below)

Suggestions:

Dark blue and plum assortment totaling about 1 yard

Assorted pea greens fat quarter

Assorted light neutrals totaling 1/2 yard

Assorted medium neutrals such as tan, gray, tan plaid, etc. – totaling 1/2 yard

Black 1/8 yard

Scraps red and medium blue

Hooking supplies

Cutting/Assembly

Transfer of pattern: the pattern provided is only for the 'ovals" area. The overall rug is 31" wide x 29" high. Draw borders this size, the ovals fit into the center leaving about 4" on each side to fill with the background and the 2 rows of loops. I tear my strips into about 3/4" strips unless the wool does not tear. Then I cut it, and then cut up the center of this strip to make 2 strips. This gives the rugs a more primitive look. With this method you can vary the widths of your strip, cutting narrow slivers as needed.

Finish the rug as you wish.

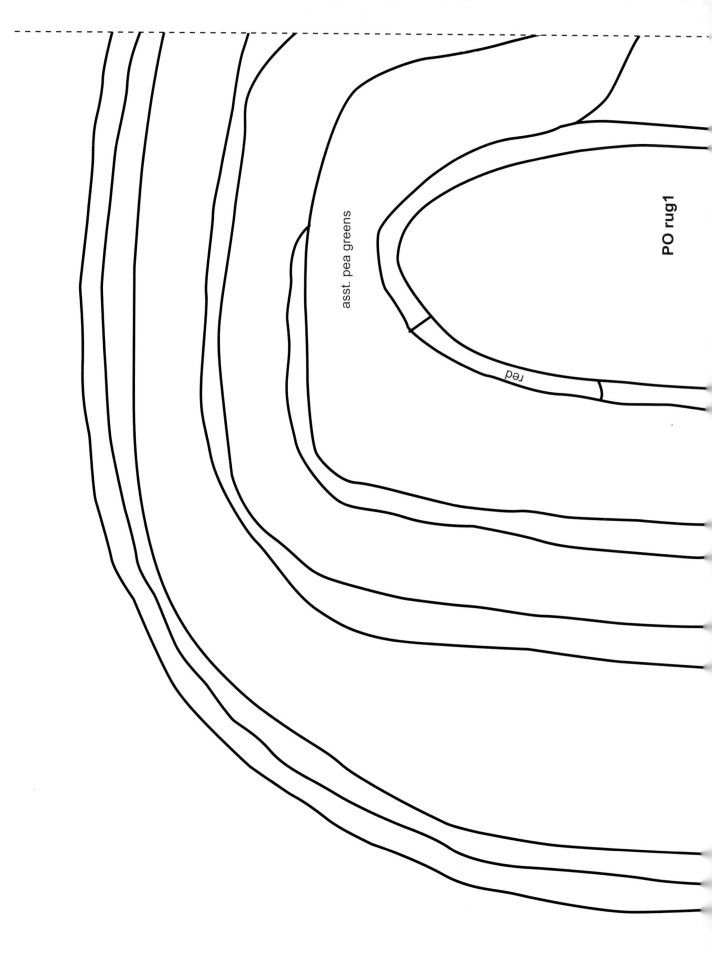

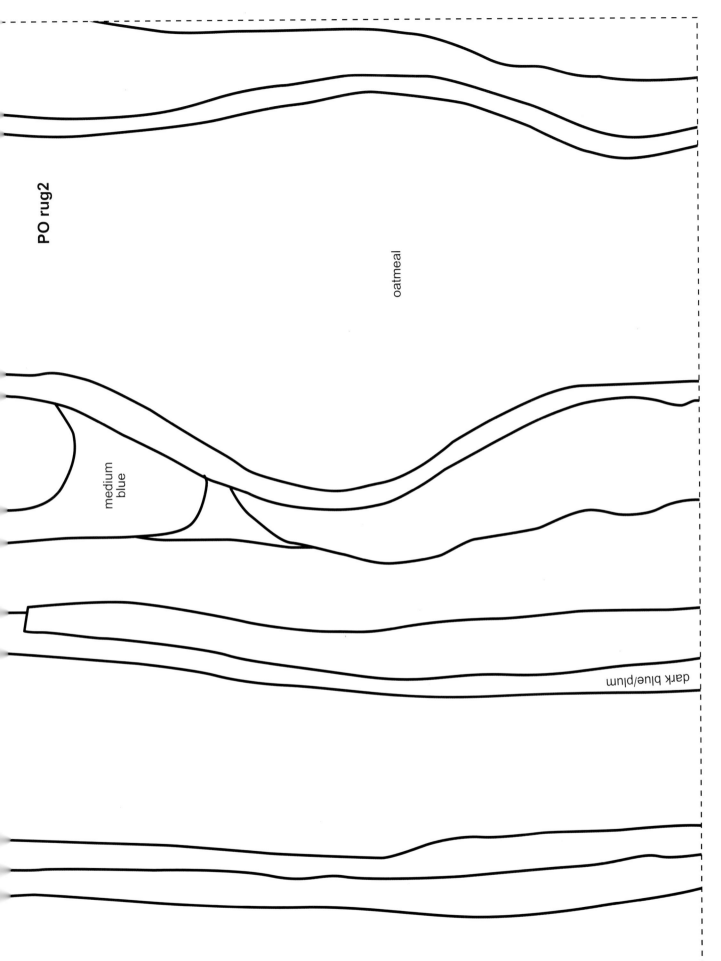

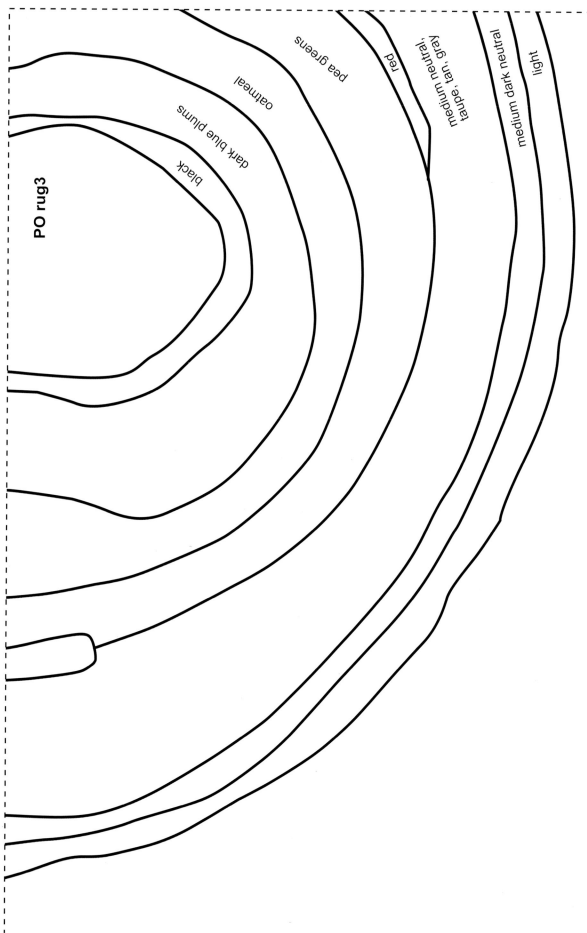

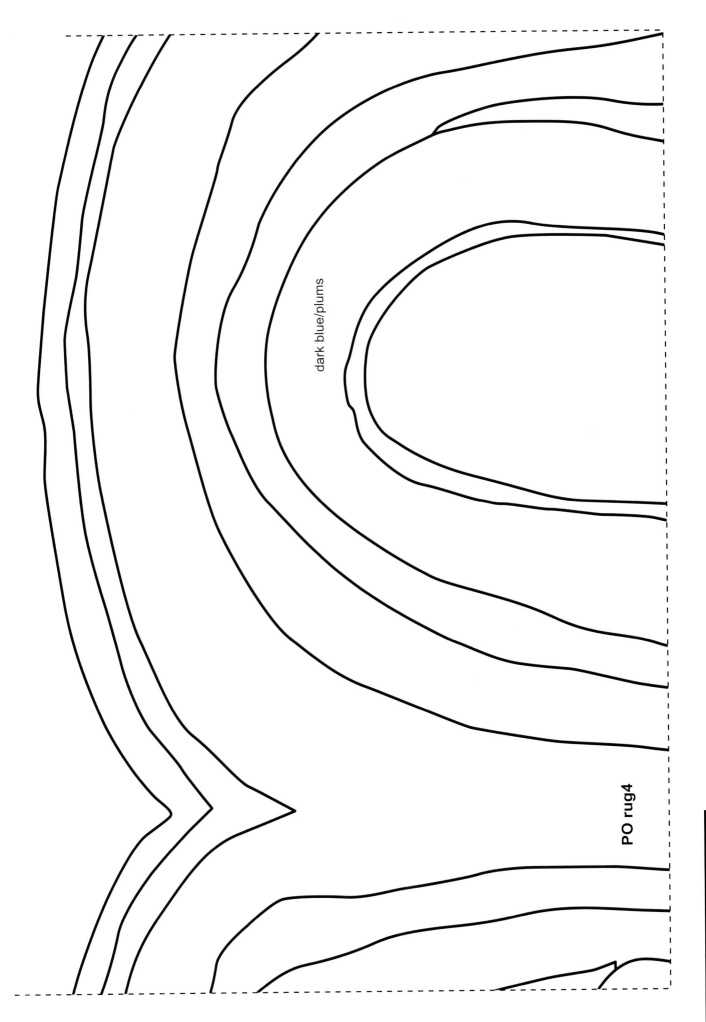

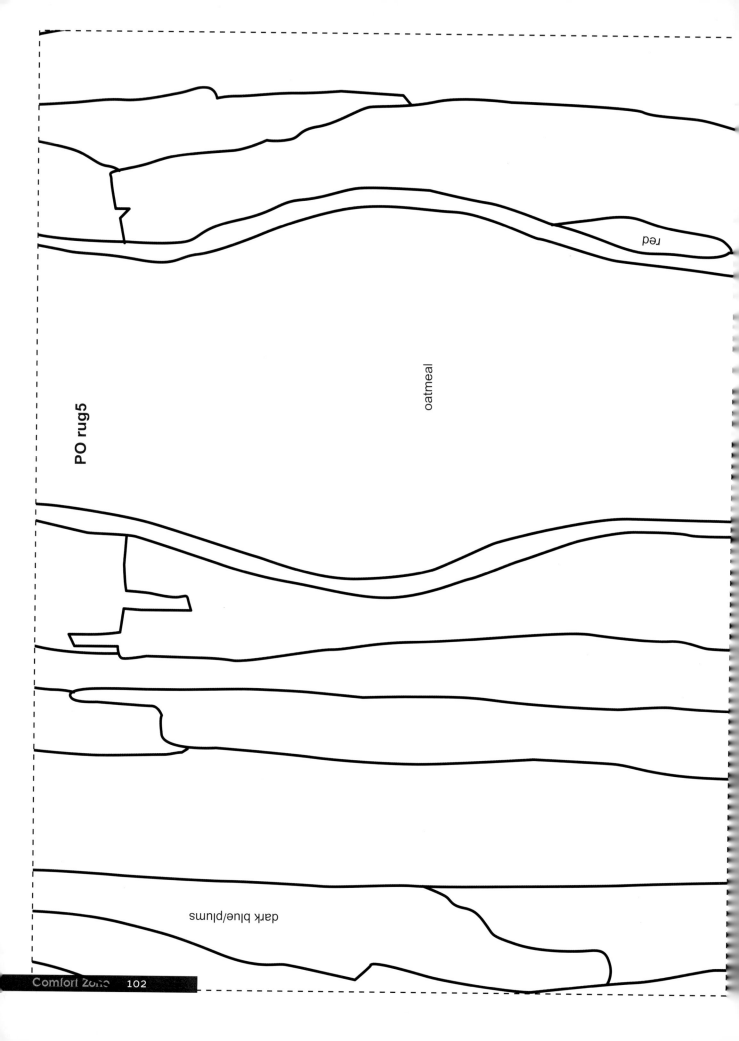

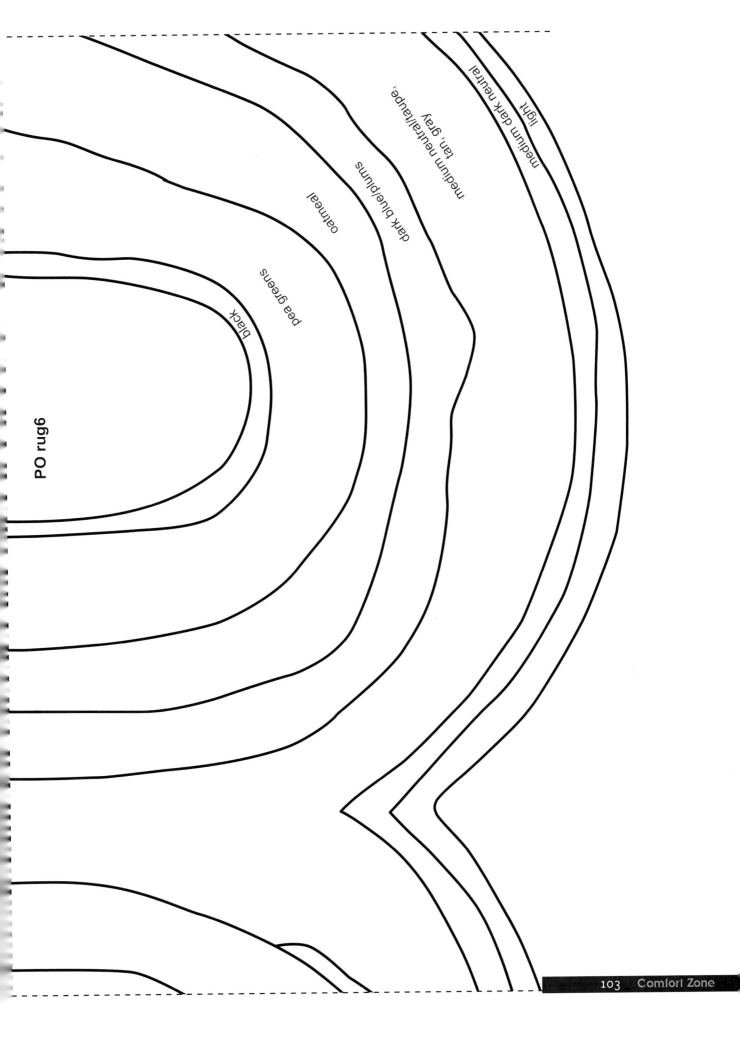

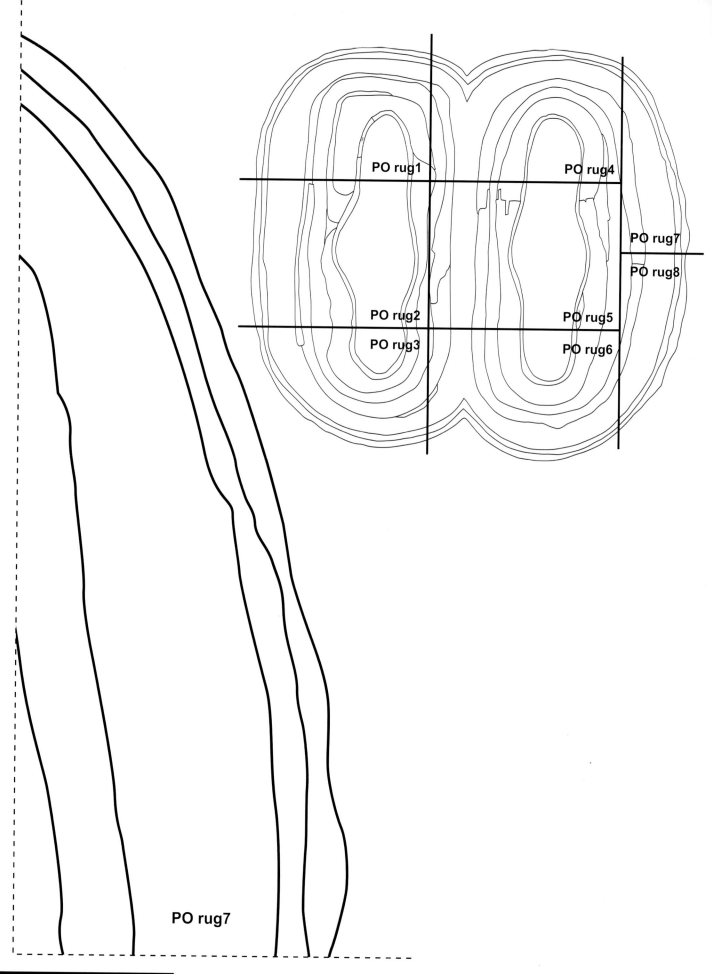

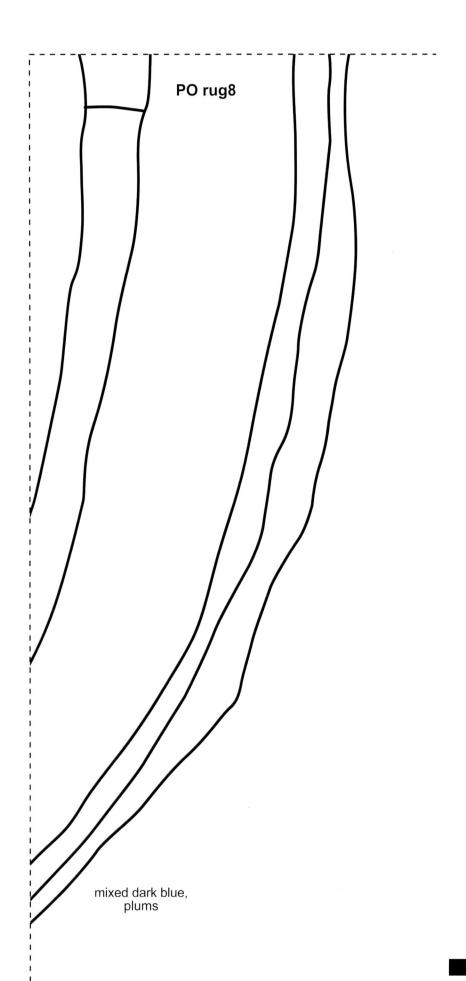

27" x 33"

This hooked rug was inspired by one I bought that had some damage. I liked the colors. Some of the dark blues were fading to plum - I am not sure the other colors changed much. The rug isn't even square but there is a square on point in the center. I love old hooked rugs, hooked without worrying about perfect loops or whether they twisted on top or bottom, things we try to avoid today while hooking. Old rugs often needed to cover the floor and the design was made from whatever fabric was available. If Pa's coat wasn't worn out yet, it wouldn't be included even if it was a color you wanted! I think because of the limited colors of old used clothes, women (and men) were very good at creating a design. Geometric designs were common on utility rugs.

Fabric requirements and supplies

Monks cloth or linen 41" x 35" foundation for pattern

Assorted dark wool totaling approximately 1 1/2 yards

Example of dark colors: blue gray, dark navy, plum, brown, black, gray

Assorted light wools totaling approximately 1 1/2 yards

Example of light wools: oatmeal, light gray, tan, woven tan plaids

Your frame and hook of choice

Transfer the pattern on page 109 to linen or monks cloth. Use the diagram to divide the pattern into sections. First divide it in quarters - outside dimensions are 33" wide x 27" high. Draw a line 1 1/2" in from outer edge. Use the diagram to draw additional sections and use the photo for color planning.

Cutting/Assembly

I used a wide strip. I tear a strip of wool about 3/4" wide then cut up the center of the strip. You will need to hook with a larger hook. What I did with this rug was pull up my loops without worrying if they were straight or crossed in the back - it gives the rug a more primitive and old look. I really like this look and it was quick to hook, giving the rows a wobbly appearance. I think if everything was just perfect it would look more contemporary. I think everyone should step out of their comfortable, carefully learned comfort zone and try it. It was a fun rug to make and the end result is a great primitive rug.

Comfort Zone 108

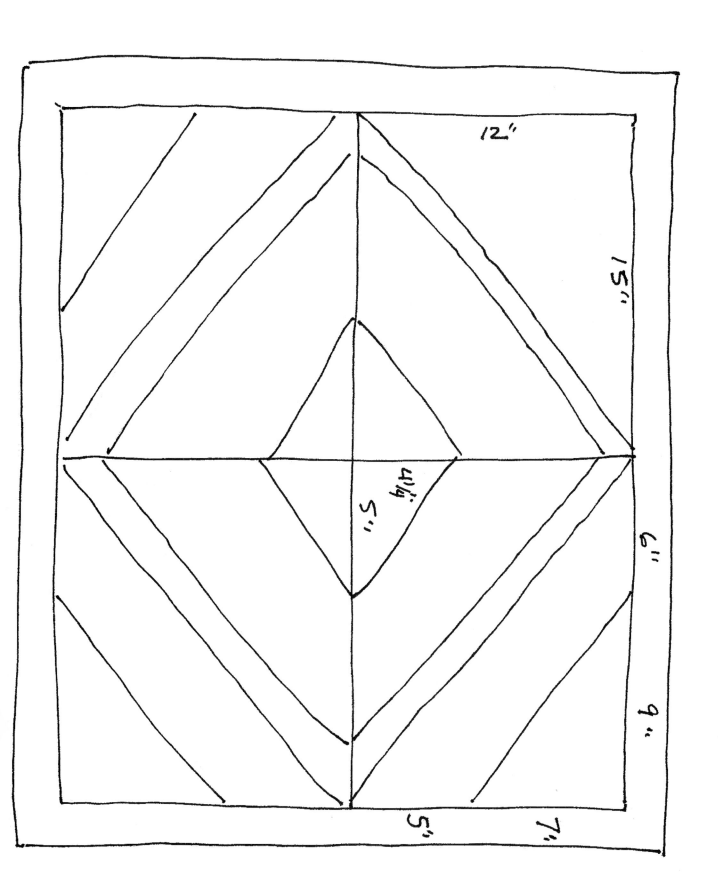

Resources

Listed in projects

Sand filled Pins, a useful pincushion, page 73
Parakeet gravel and grit can be found in pet stores. This is easier to work with than a 50-pound bag of sand.

Quilt Shops: fabric, wool, and cross stitch supplies

Country Sampler
133 East Jefferson St.
Spring Green, WI 53588
608-588-2510
sgcountrysampler.com

Quilters Station
3680 NE Akin Dr
Lee's Summit, MO 64064
816-525-8955
quiltersstation.com

The Buggy Barn
28848 Tramm Rd N
Reardan, WA 99029
509-796-2188
buggybarnquilts.com

Rug Hooking supplies

Emma Lou Lais
Emma Lou's Primitives
5015 Chouteau St.
Shawnee, KS 66226
913-745-5605
emmalousprimitives.com

Rhonda Manley
16221 NE 116 St.
Liberty, MO 64068
816-781-6844
rhonda@blacksheepwooldesigns.com
www.blacksheepwooldesigns.com

Blackberry Primitives
Cindi 402-423-8464
Tonja 402-261-8165
www.blackberryprimitives.com
Wool@Blackberryprimitives.com

Anita White
12835 Perry
Overland Park, KS 66213
913-685-0180
anitahooksrugs@yahoo.com

Rustic Rugs
Judy Cripps
3212 SW Arrowhead Rd.
Topeka, KS 66614
785-273-2093
www.judycripps.com
rusticrugs@judycripps.com

Saltbox Primitive Woolens
Patty Wallace
30148 West Dam Access Rd.
Warsaw, MO 65355
660-438-6002
saltboxwoolens@embarqmail.com
www.saltboxwoolens.com

Black Horse Antiques
Janice Lee
29049 Garvin Road
Valley, NE 68064
402-359-2699
www.janicelee.biz
info@janicelee.biz

Baskets of Wool
Cammie Bruce
Lincoln, NE
402-742-3071
basketsofwool@alltel.net
www.basketsofwool.com

Simply Butternut
Maggie Bonanomi
1006 Highland Dr.
Lexington, MO 64067
660-232-4406
maggiebonanomi@juno.com

Antique Shops: old blankets, fabrics and antiques

Bruce Burstert LLC
1010 Main St., lower level
Lexington, MO 64067
Bruce Burstert: 816-665-7989
Carl Wheat 816-257-2222

Missouri River Antique Co.
912 Main St.
Lexington, MO 64067
660-259-3097

Greenwood Mercantile
409 Main
Greenwood, MO 64034
816-537-7033

Country Heritage & Friends
16005 Allendale Lake Rd.
Greenwood, MO 64034
816-537-8863
816-537-7822

Friends Together Antiques
203 N Central St.
Rocheport, MO 65279
Fri & Sat 10-5
Amanda Canter
home 573-796-2545
  cell 573-864-4684
Carolyn Green
home 573-782-4449
  cell 573-690-7229

White Horse Antiques, rug hooking
505 Third St.
Rocheport, MO 65279
573-698-2088

I remember I remember
The house where I was born,
The little window where the sun
came peeping in the morn.

Thomas Hood
1827